TRENDS OF FEDERALISM
IN THEORY AND PRACTICE

Trends of Federalism in Theory and Practice

CARL J. FRIEDRICH

FREDERICK A. PRAEGER, *Publishers*

New York • Washington • London

FREDERICK A. PRAEGER, PUBLISHERS
111 Fourth Avenue, New York, N.Y. 10003, U.S.A.
5, Cromwell Place, London S.W.7, England

Published in the United States of America in 1968
by Frederick A. Praeger, Inc., Publishers

© 1968 by Frederick A. Praeger, Inc.

Library of Congress Catalog Card Number: 68–23352

Printed in the United States of America

Luis Muñoz Marín

In Friendship and Admiration

Neither of a man nor of a people can
a change be demanded which breaks the
unity and continuity of the personality.

UNAMUNO

PREFACE

THESE STUDIES ARE an enlarged and revised version of the essay
I contributed to the *Selected Studies* published by the United
States/Puerto Rico Status Commission in 1966; they then
bore the title *Selected Trends and Issues in Contemporary
Federal and Regional Relations.* I have included a revised
version of an article I contributed to *Government and Opposition,* Volume I (1966). I have also added to chapter 3 material from my contribution to the issue of *Orbis* dedicated to
Hans Kohn (January, 1967). Finally, I have revised and incorporated in chapter 2 a paper I originally prepared for the
United States Information Service and which has since been
published by *Jahrbuch des Öffentlichen Rechts,* whose re-
nowned editor, Gerhard Leibholz, has for years been interested in comparative federalism. I hope that these studies may
help in furthering the continued discussion and exploration
of federalism. It is a vast and ever expanding field, and yet
one in which many important issues remain to be more fully
explored, and in which ever new and often surprising experience is being gathered in old and new states.

When Arthur MacMahon edited his fine collection *Federalism: Mature and Emergent* (1955), he introduced it with
a highly significant and balanced statement of the perspectives
which had by then become distinctly visible. In a way, these
papers were a very helpful companion to *Studies in Federal-*

ism (1954), which Robert R. Bowie and I had edited and which focused attention upon the process of policy formation. This we did at the urging of Paul-Henri Spaak, who, as president of the *Ad Hoc* Assembly, feared that this distinguished gathering of Europeans engaged in the task of drafting a constitution for a European political community would become bogged down in sterile discussions of structure and, more particularly, in the issue of sovereignty, unless their attention was directed toward the actual governing and policy-making of operating federal systems: Australia, Canada, Germany, Switzerland, and the United States.

Since that time, federal theory and practice have significantly advanced, and some dramatic failures of federalism have been witnessed (Nigeria, the Caribbean Federation, Maphilindo, and others). Very serious strains have developed in some of the mature federal systems, notably Canada and the United States. Hence the questioning continues, but, even in the erstwhile totalitarian regimes, notably Yugoslavia, federalism continues to develop new potentialities. Wherever democratization and industrialization reach an advanced stage, the demand for effective decentralization and/or federalization becomes insistent, as new groups discover their distinctive identity. Short of general anarchy, federalizing such communities appears to be the only solution: sometimes in the interest of greater unity, at other times in the interest of greater diversity. To high-light some of the issues and to delineate possible conclusions from the experience that is being developed are the purposes of this volume.

What I have here gathered together lies beyond the institutional and structural field, which is reviewed in my new chapter on federalism in the revised edition of *Constitutional Government and Democracy* (1968), and for which Kenneth C. Wheare provided a classic statement in his *Federal Government* (1953). Social forces, societal substructures, innovations—these are here selectively adumbrated. There is one further dimension which seems to be increasingly challenging: federal behavior. What actually occurs in communities that become involved in federalizing? With a group of research associates, I am engaged in studies exploring this dimension for the Community of the Six and, especially, for France and Germany; the first volume has appeared. These explorations of the political implications of informal community-formation are continuing, with the much appreciated support of the Center for International Affairs at Harvard University and the Institut für Politische Wissenschaft at Heidelberg University. I wish to thank the directors of both these bodies for their generous assistance and encouragement. I also wish to express my appreciation to my secretary, Miss Rosalind Cummings, for her devoted labors in the vineyard, and the editor at Praeger, Mrs. Marian Wood, for her many helpful bits of advice, and her patience. Similarly, the periodic gatherings of students of federalism under the inspired guidance of Denis de Rougemont at his *Centre d'Etudes Européennes* at Geneva over the last few years have helped to deepen my appreciation of the vast range and complexity of the federal world problem. Finally, I should like to add that my collaborators in the several meetings of the International Political Science Association who contributed papers and participated in discussions, especially at Oxford, Geneva, and Brussels, have been a source of great stimulation. This work is going forward at the present time under a committee ably presided over by M. Rabier.

May I hope that the old Roman adage will be applied to these pages: *dum desint vires, tamen est laudanda voluntas.*

CARL J. FRIEDRICH

Harvard University
September, 1968

CONTENTS

PART III: THEORETICAL TRENDS

PART I

General Problems

1

THE THEORY OF FEDERALISM
AS PROCESS

A CONCRETE POLITICAL ORDER may operate on several levels of
community: local, regional, national, or supranational. In
speaking of such "levels" one suggests that they are sharply
separated from each other, like boxes piled on top of one another. Actually, levels of community and government are
never thus sharply divided; they constantly interact, as the
human beings operating them argue, fight, cooperate, and
compromise with one another. Still, to speak of "levels of government" has a distinct and operational meaning, namely the
range or territorial extension of power and authority. There
are five such levels that are generally recognized, though there
could be more. These five levels are constituted by the community to which the level refers: the local community, the
tribal or regional community, the national community, the
supranational cultural, and the global world community.[1]

The contemporary world is significantly shaped by complex
patterns of interaction between these several kinds of communities. Federalism, regionalism, and decentralization have all
increased in importance as possible ways of dealing with the

3

political issues resulting from such interaction. Federalism can be viewed as little more than a particular form of decentralization.[2] From a strictly administrative standpoint there is much to be said for thus interpreting federalism. But, as the word decentralization clearly indicates, such an approach posits the center as given and primary, and allows for subcenters as, in effect, governmental entities to which some power and authority have been delegated for purely pragmatic and heuristic reasons. This is in fact often an unrealistic assumption to make. Either the subcenters may be primary, as were the Swiss cantons, or they may be coeval, as was the case with the American states. If this situation is recurrent in federal relations, it is equally true of regional relations. In spite of the prepotency of the central government in France, the historic regions in France have preserved a measure of real community. Not only Brittany and Alsace, but also Provence and Flanders have a distinctive personality, though it is not at present institutionalized, as the regionalist movement has demanded for years it should be. In Italy, since World War II, regionalism has achieved constitutional protection; not only Sicily, but also the other border regions have been recognized as distinctive, and a regional division of the country has been embodied in the constitution, albeit weakly and ineffectively. Such regionalism is not the result of administrative and governmental convenience; quite the contrary. It has occurred in response to the surviving vigor of distinctive regional ways of life and traditions rooted in a distant tribal and historical past.

Regionalism has frequently been associated with tribalism. That is especially the case in some of the new nations. Even a constitutional document as sophisticated as that of the Weimar Republic spoke in its preamble of "the German people, united in its tribes." These tribal communities, whether in Germany, in India, or in Nigeria, are reinforced by marked linguistic peculiarities, whether these be merely dialects, as in Germany, or wholly distinct languages, as in India. It was a characteristic feature of the old empires that they allowed such cultural regionalism wide scope. Czarist Russia, Austria-Hungary, and the Ottoman Empire were quite willing to acknowledge the existence of such regional communities of language and culture, and the same was true of oriental empires.[3] Such acknowledgement went hand in hand with a vigorous and often oppressive centralization of administration of those functions which concerned the central imperial power. It is a tradition which the Soviet Union has continued with considerable skill, even while insisting that their policy was motivated by quite different considerations, rooted in Marxist ideology. Indeed, Soviet "federalism" is basically a legal recognition of the tribally determined regionalism of its polyethnic population base.

Decentralization may, on the other hand, be largely unrelated to distinctive community formation. The constitutional tradition of English local self-government is community-based; but the French *départements* were fixed with "ruler and compass," utterly disregarding past tradition and local communal bonds. To be sure, decentralization in France has been of very limited scope; but there has been an increasing amount of it, resulting from the needs of a more and more complex pattern of governmental tasks, as well as popular pressures, operating through democratic channels.

If one were to contrast federalism and decentralization, as is often done in political studies, the conclusion is rather equivocal. At times unitary government is simply thought of as centralized government, and then contrasted with federal systems, leaving entirely out of account the possibility that a unitary government may be decentralized, as it is in England and was in Prussia. Are there no distinctions between such a decentralized government and a federal one? Is it merely a matter of the "territorial composition of the state"? Of decentralized England it has been said that "the British system is nevertheless dominated by the idea that all legislative power is presumed to lie in the first instance in the King in Parliament and all executive power in the Crown—a twofold constitutional principle which represents the very apotheosis of centralization."⁴ Is this an accurate assessment? What is really centralized is the power over legislation and its execution, surely a vast area of governmental functions, but one hedged in by English constitutional tradition. A vital part of this tradition is that of local self-government and of the decentralization which that tradition implies. It is so deeply embedded in the pattern of English constitutionalism that any frontal attack upon it would be sharply resented; yet the centralizing tendencies have eaten away a good part of its foundations. Newer constitutions, embodied in a more or less systematic document, have therefore undertaken to "guarantee" such decentralization through explicit protection of local self-government.⁵ When that occurs, the situation is similar to that of a constitutionally protected regionalism. How are both to be distinguished from federalism? The question does not permit, as already indicated, a clear and unequivocal answer. It is possible, however, to approximate a meaningful distinction, if one recalls that a federal order typically preserves the institutional and behavioral features of a *foedus,* a compact between equals to act jointly on specific issues of general policy. Effective separate representation of the component units for the purpose of participating in legislation and the shaping of public policy, and, more especially, effective separate representation in the amending of the constitutional charter itself may be said to provide reasonably precise criteria for a federal as contrasted with a merely decentralized order of government. Whether under particular conditions one or the other arrangement is more appropriate constitutes a problem of practical politics which can only be solved in terms of the specific situation. Generally speaking, it can be said that decentralization is indicated where functional considerations are of primary importance, whereas communal preoccupation demands a federal system. There is no object in laboring the distinction, which is clear enough when Switzerland and England are juxtaposed.

Decentralization has, however, a particular meaning in connection with some federal systems. In these systems, the administrative execution of federal legislation is placed in the hands of the component units as is done in Switzerland, Austria, and the Federal Republic of Germany. This form of decentralization is of such importance in contemporary federalism that we shall deal with it in separate chapters. (See chapters 8 and 17.) Suffice it here to say that such decentralization is intended to reinforce the federal system and does in fact do so.

In the light of the foregoing, it is possible to define federalism and federal relations in dynamic terms. The problems connected with such a definition will be more fully explored later (see chapters 2 and 23), but it seems at the outset desirable to stress that federalism should not be seen only as a static pattern or design, characterized by a particular and precisely fixed division of powers between governmental levels. Federalism is also and perhaps primarily the process of federalizing a political community, that is to say, the process by which a number of separate political communities enter into arrangements for working out solutions, adopting joint policies, and making joint decisions on joint problems, and, conversely, also the process by which a unitary political community becomes differentiated into a federally organized whole. Federal relations are fluctuating relations in the very nature of things. Any federally organized community must therefore provide itself with instrumentalities for the recurrent revision of its pattern or design. For only thus can the shifting balance of common and disparate values, interests, and beliefs be effectively reflected in more differentiated or more integrated relations. In short, we have federalism only if a set of political communities coexist and interact as autonomous entities, united in a common order with an autonomy of its own. No sovereign can exist in a federal system; autonomy and sovereignty exclude each other in such a political order. To speak of the transfer of part of the sovereignty is to deny the idea of sovereignty which since Bodin has meant indivisibility. No one has the "last word." The idea of a compact is inherent in federalism, and the "constituent power," which makes the compact, takes the place of the sovereign.[6]

In the light of the foregoing, the ongoing discussion in America about the passing of "dual" federalism, about "cooperative" and, now, "creative" federalism are quite in keeping with what to expect. The very vitality of American federalism is the result of its continuing adaptation to changing circumstances. Recently, it has been suggested—and supported with good arguments—that there are four stages in the evolution of American federalism: first, a marked "dualism" which could be called "state mercantilism" (1790–1860); second, a centralizing federalism (1860–1933); third, the New Deal's "cooperative" federalism extending until very recently; and fourth, the "creative" federalism of the last few years.[7] Patently, these dramatic changes serve to illustrate both the integrating and the differentiating potential of the federalizing process. They do not at all exclude a measure of genuine continuity which surely is there.[8] In order to appreciate this stable core, we shall turn to the origin and development of the concept of dynamic federalism, in the following chapter.

Here it remains to say a word about the general literature on federalism. As a recent careful bibliography stated, "unfortunately there exists no general treatise on federalism."[9] It added that "the nearest thing to a treatise proper is by a distinguished Indian scholar, B. M. Sharma."[10] I am not sure that it is a bad thing that we do not have such a treatise. In any case, the present study makes no pretense at being a treatise. It seeks to illuminate various features and problems, as have previous writings of the author. And so do the many studies in federalism which have been published since *The Federalist* started modern writings in the field. These writings are either country-oriented or problem-oriented. A critical bibliography of both dimensions is one of the most urgent research needs.

NOTES TO CHAPTER 1

1. For a discussion of the general theoretical aspects of political community, see my *Man and His Government* (1963), chapter 8; for the problem of levels, *ibid.*, chapter 29 *passim* and the literature cited there. For the empirical data, see R. R. Bowie and C. J. Friedrich (eds.), *Studies in Federalism* (1954). See also my general reports to the Oxford Round Table (1963) and to the Geneva Congress of the International Political Science Association (IPSA), entitled respectively "Federalism, National and International" and "New Tendencies in Federal Theory and Practice"; the former was published in German in *Politische Vierteljahrsschrift* (1964), the latter, in English, in *Jahrbuch des Öffentlichen Rechts* (New Series, Vol. 14 (1965).

2. Decentralization has become a widespread goal, because of the tendency toward overcentralization; on this, see J. R. Pennock, *Liberal Democracy* (1950), p. 178, and my *Constitutional Government and Democracy* (4th ed.; 1968), chapter XI. The subject in its ramifications constituted one of the major topics of the Sixth World Congress of IPSA (Geneva Congress) in 1964, because it is also a major concern of the Soviet Union; on this, see Alfred G. Meyer, *The Soviet Political System* (1966), pp. 256 ff.

3. See S. N. Eisenstadt, *The Political Systems of Empires—The Rise and Fall of the Historical Bureaucratic Societies* (1962), and Richard Koebner, *Empire* (1961, 1965), pp. 281 ff.

4. W. A. Robson, *The Development of Local Government* (1948), p. 189.

5. See Italian constitution (1948), Article 5; Constitution of the Federal Republic of Germany (1949), Article 28(2); Constitution of Bavaria (1947), Article 11; Constitution of Baden-Württemberg (1947), Article 98.

6. On this difficult point, see my *op. cit.* (note 2 above), chapter VIII.

7. Harry N. Scheiber, "The Condition of American Federalism: An Historian's View," a study submitted by the Subcommittee on Intergovernmental Relations to the Committee on Government Operations, U.S. Senate, October 15, 1966 (89th Congress).

8. Scheiber takes sharp issue with the views of Morton Grodzins and Daniel Elazar when they—in the studies cited below—project the tendency toward "sharing" backward into nineteenth-century American federalism. While I agree with him on the specific point, I believe that continuity is not a fallacy, but implied in Scheiber's own argument. See also for this continuity Arthur E. Sutherland, *Constitutionalism in America—Origin and Development of Its Fundamental Ideas* (1965), especially chapter 13, which portrays what Sutherland rightly calls "the decline of State Independence" in the period prior to 1865. For the views of Grodzins and Elazar, see Morton Grodzins, *The American System*, ed. Daniel Elazar (1966), especially chapter 2.

9. *Federalism in the Commonwealth*, ed. William S. Livingston (1963), es-

pecially p. 1. Livingston has himself contributed a good essay on general works, though unfortunately it does not significantly go back beyond Freeman, and it overestimates some studies of "conventional wisdom" in the field. It is notably culture-bound in its preoccupation with writings in English.

10. B. M. Sharma, *Federalism in Theory and Practice* (2 vols., 1951). Based upon a static view. Another traditional view was expounded in K. C. Wheare's widely read *Federal Government* (1946, 3d ed., 1953). It should be noted, though, that in contrast to frequent statements to the contrary, Wheare did not undertake to treat federalism, but federal *government*.

2

THE ORIGIN AND DEVELOPMENT OF THE CONCEPT

FEDERALISM IS FREQUENTLY SPOKEN OF as an American invention. And this is a correct statement if the particular kind of union created in 1787 is taken as the archetype of federalism. For nowhere before had so close a union been combined with so much freedom (or autonomy) of the component parts. Past attempts at federal union had usually remained at the level of a league or long-term alliance. The nearest parallels in European history were the Swiss Confederation and the United Provinces of the Netherlands, both referred to in *The Federalist*, but the first had not achieved an effective central government, while, in the second, the component units languished for lack of autonomy. The problem was later formalized by German jurists who developed the dichotomy of *Staatenbund* and *Bundesstaat*—a distinction which has dominated much thought on federalism ever since. The builders of the American Constitution were happily unconcerned with so abstract an argument. Being men of practical affairs, they saw the situation as it concretely confronted them: the Confederation with its lack of adequate central government and its need for more effective union. It was a question of more or less, not of either-or, and they proceeded to deal with the situation in such pragmatic terms. From this experience, theorists have been slow to learn that federalism is a process rather than a static pattern.

Neither Plato nor Aristotle, nor the many political writers following in their footsteps in classical antiquity, developed a concept of federalism. The repeated attempts at federalism which were made to unite Greece against Macedonia and Rome failed. It was only in the Middle Ages, with its great city leagues, that the first vague hints at such a concept appeared. But not until the confederations of the Swiss and Dutch had come into being did a full-bodied concept of federalism make its appearance. This concept was formulated by Johannes Althusius (1562–1638), who, fully conversant with both these federal regimes, made the bond of union (*consociatio*) one of the cornerstones of his political thought. In contrast to Jean Bodin (1530–1596)—who is justly celebrated for establishing the concept of sovereignty, but precisely for that reason was hard put to give an adequate account of the emergent federal government of Switzerland or of the federally organized Empire—Althusius expounded a federal theory of popular sovereignty.[1]

In his celebrated *Politica* (1603, 1610), he built his federal union upon a supporting hierarchy of lesser unions. On successive levels of community, from the family to the state (*regnum*), he held that those who live together and whom he called "symbiotics" are united by a pact, express or implied, to share things in pursuit of common interests and utility. The village was for him a federal union of families—as was the guild—the town a union of guilds, the province a union of towns, villages, and the like, the kingdom or state a union of such provinces, and the empire a union of such states and free cities. In a sense, this was a concept which transformed the feudal hierarchy of successive levels of lords and vassals, as mirrored in

Dante, Thomas Aquinas, and other medieval writers, into a modern constitutional one. The key to this concept of federalism is that on all levels the union is composed of the units of the preceding lower level, so that when we arrive at the top, the members of a state are neither individual persons nor families, guilds, or other such lower communities, but only the provinces and free cities. This puts the Althusian concept in sharp contrast to the later American concept, which sees the federal union composed of individual persons as well as of states. Grotius, though sharply opposed to Althusius's idea of popular sovereignty, shared this concept of federal union. Writing specifically against the background of the Netherlands, he too sees the political commonwealth as a perpetual union of lesser communities, united through *consociatio,* or union.[2]

No significant development of the concept of federalism occurred in the century and a half following Althusius's bold theory. Hobbes and Locke saw the state purely in terms of individuals and they were followed in this by Spinoza and Leibniz as well as Pufendorf, who denounced the quaint federal body of the decaying empire as a "monstrosity." It was only in connection with the longing for a universal order of peace that the notion of an all-inclusive federal union continued to play a certain role, from Henry IV's Grand Design to the Abbé de Saint-Pierre's (1658–1743) *Projet* (1713), but rather as a utopian future order, cast in the form of a mere league, than as a form of government. The same really holds for Montesquieu's (1689–1755) federalism; he discusses the notion of a "federative republic" in Book IX of his *Spirit of the Laws* (1748), but largely in terms of giving defensive strength to several republics. He describes such a federative republic as a convention by which several bodies politic consent to become "citizens" of a larger state. He calls it a "society of societies." As so often, Montesquieu's formulations challenge by their breadth, without being supported by his analysis.[3] Yet this analysis stresses one point which found expression in Article IV, Section 4 of the American Constitution: Federal republics ought to be composed only of republics. It is the principle of homogeneity. Montesquieu did not elaborate the institutional structure of such a federal republic, nor indeed did he analyze the institutions of past federations, except in a sketchy contrast of the Netherlands and an ancient federation, Lycia. Yet in view of the keen interest of the American "founding fathers" in Montesquieu, what little Montesquieu had to say was indubitably carefully considered. He did not present the American concept of federalism, however, any more than Althusius had done.

It is no exaggeration to say that federalism was the most central issue of the constitutional convention at Philadelphia. And what was finally adopted were institutions which its framers considered distinct innovations. In the fourteenth chapter of *The Federalist,* James Madison stated this sense of novelty very emphatically. After speaking of the "numerous innovations," he exclaims: "They [the drafters of the constitution] accomplished a Revolution which has no parallel in the annals of human society. They reared the fabrics of governments which have no model on the face of the globe."[4] There can be no doubt that this sense of innovation was especially justified in regard to federalism. It is in this field that the most important inventions were made.

The much maligned and little-studied Articles of Confederation (1781) had, however, made a significant beginning. While much more nearly in line with earlier federal thinking, they went beyond its framework. For while insisting that the several states were retaining their "sovereignty, freedom and independence," they yet proceeded not only to set up a separate federal government, but they made a first start in the direction of the idea of such a government being a government of individuals. Each citizen of any state was to share the privileges and immunities of free citizens in any other state, was to be prosecuted in any state, if a fugitive from justice, and the like. Yet, on the whole the Confederation was built on the Althusian principle of *consociatio* which made only the state a member of it. It also stuck close to Montesquieu's notion of a federative republic as one of common defense. Indeed it was Montesquieu's insistence upon the difficulty of maintaining a republican form of government over a large territory which stimulated the belief in federalism. Therefore, the governing functions attributed to the Confederation were mainly defense, foreign policy, western lands, weights and measures, trade with the Indians, posts, currency, and credit. The Articles contained no mention of a federal executive, though a judiciary was implied by its provisions for the judicial functions of the federal congress. No direct taxing power was provided for the Confederation.[5]

So loosely constructed a federalism could not hope to deal effectively with the task confronting young America. Economic crisis, political confusion, and the danger of losing their newly won independence soon confronted the Americans. Much searching practical thought was given to the federalism which had been adopted under the Articles of Confederation. Yet, not the concept of federalism as such, but the concrete issues of government operation were the focus of attention. When finally, after some very skillful moves of the outstanding advocates of stronger union, especially Madison and Hamilton, the convention met in Philadelphia, it was composed of men of many shades of opinion concerning the problems we now recognize as those of federalism, but there was not one among them who was an academic theorist on federalism, not one who had preconceived notions as to its "true" nature.

In fact, the concept was hammered out in a protracted struggle between two dominant factions of the convention,[6] the nationalists and the federalists (not to be confused with the Federalist party which grew out of the nationalists). Of these the first had formulated and set forth their conception in the so-called Virginia Plan, which would have given the federal Congress the power to legislate in all matters which it wished to take up because of failure of the states to do it. They even would have had the federal legislature veto state laws and coerce the states by military force, if necessary. The federalists, by contrast, though ready to form a stronger union than had existed under the Confederation, were solicitous of states' prerogatives. The New Jersey Plan which they offered to the convention contained many provisions that were eventually to become part of the American concept. It strictly circumscribed the federal legislative powers and looked to the judiciary for over-all review of both state and federal legislation. But the federalists failed to provide for national representation, and the executive they proposed would have been quite weak. The new federalism emerged as a compromise between those who were prepared to give the national government limitless superiority, entrusting the federal legislature with the power to interpret the constitution at will, and those who would keep the federal government weak in order to protect the autonomy of the several states. In finding this compromise, a middle group, who might be called unionists, were very important. With little dogmatism and much careful attention to practical detail, the two opposed views were merged in a new concept of federalism which combined a strong, presidential executive, two houses of Congress of which one represented the nation and the other the states, a judicial guardian of the federal constitution, and, after the first ten amendments were passed, a broad guarantee of civil rights and liberties for the citizen in his dealings with federal (and eventually state) authorities. It was a concept not limited to defense and security as the purpose and end of federal union; rather, it envisaged a national economy which was to become the real foundation of the American nation.

The arguments at Philadelphia were consequently focused upon the specific issues of governmental pattern. Just the same, the debates were dominated by the federal problems: How to divide legislative power between the states and the federal government, how to balance the fields of governmental activity so as to produce a sound equilibrium between states and nation, how to arrange matters so as not to favor either the large or the small states unduly, and so forth. From these debates, carried on by men of principle who yet had a very sound sense of practical necessities, there emerged a *novel, unprecedented concept of federalism.* It rests upon the notion that in a federal system of government, each citizen belongs to two communities, that of his state and that of the nation; that these two levels of community should be clearly distinguished and effectively provided each with their own government; and that in the structuring of the government of the larger community the component states as states must play a distinctive role. Contrary to the earlier notions, as found in Althusius and others, the federal system here is not composed merely of states, as is a league, but creates a new community, all-inclusive, of the citizens of all the states. This new conception is particularly tangible in the fiscal arrangements which give to both the states and the nation separate and distinct tax resources of their own, and it pervades the entire Constitution, its provisions for citizenship, for defense, and the rest. It is part of the practice which has developed under this concept of federalism that there exist two separate levels of administration, the state and the federal level, and that each is operating independently of the other. It is another striking feature of the American concept of federalism that the federal government exercises only those functions specifically assigned to it, while the states have what is known as the residual powers. This notion, which goes back to the Articles of Confederation, was meant to restrict the federal sphere. But, due to judicial interpretation and the breadth of the terms employed to describe federal functions, such as "interstate commerce," it has, in the course of time, become almost the opposite, namely a basis for steadily expanding federal powers. The role of the judicial power and, more especially, the Supreme Court in fostering this development was not envisaged by the drafters of the Constitution, who believed, with Montesquieu, that the judicial power is "in a certain sense nothing." It has, however, in the course of time, become a paramount feature of the American concept of federalism, and if one consults the relevant portions of *The Federalist,* it is evident that Hamilton foresaw this evolution to some extent at least.

The Federalist is, to a large extent, the theoretical statement of the new concept of federalism which the Constitution embodied. Written by Hamilton, with the help of Madison and Jay, to defend the Constitution during the struggle for its adoption, *The Federalist* has ever since been recognized as the bible of American federalism,[7] and has consequently exercised an enormous influence in the shaping of federal institutions all over the world. Switzerland and Germany, Canada and Australia, India and a host of other countries have studied the elaborate arguments which Hamilton developed to explain the new concept, have adopted, adapted, and developed, as well as at times rejected the basic features of it. The American concept, at this point, may be called the discovery of the "federal state," because that was the term which the Germans and others attached to it when they contrasted it to a confederation of states. Actually, no such dichotomy was ever faced by the master builders of the American system. They were, in fact, the first who realized, at least in part, that federalism is not a fixed and static pattern, but a process. They provided for the amendment of their constitution, but they did it in such a way that the federal concept was fully embodied in the amending provisions, both states and nation participating fully in any such amendment.

The Federalist rightly pointed with pride to this "protection" of the states against federal invasion of their sphere.

Generally speaking, *The Federalist* built its theoretical defense of the new concept of federalism, as it had been worked out at Philadelphia, on two basic propositions. The first of these was concerned with the end of a federal union and argued that it was the *safety* of its citizens from external attack and internal tyranny. The second was focused on the need for a federal government sufficiently *strong* to carry out its functions. That this second proposition might well clash with the second part of the first proposition was readily granted by the authors. To cope with this danger, they adopted the doctrine of the separation of powers, as developed by Montesquieu, though modified by the Lockean tradition and practical experience in the colonies. *The Federalist* does not really add to but rather elaborates the concept of federalism which the convention had evolved. This is the reason that the American judiciary were able to refer to *The Federalist* as the most important commentary on the Constitution, providing primary evidence on how various difficult clauses might be interpreted.

This American view of the federal order as composed of two sharply separated spheres later came to be known as "dual federalism." While no longer a realistic description of the actual working of American federalism in which cooperation has replaced competition to a considerable extent (see chapter 1), it still continues as part of the constitutional "myth."

Amendments were soon sought and put through by those who had argued that the Constitution was defective because it contained no bill of rights restricting the exercise of governmental power by the federal government. Hamilton had answered that it contained a number of such rights, more especially *habeas corpus,* and that the granting of others would be dangerous, inasmuch as it would create a presumption that the government could, for example, invade the freedom of the press. But the defenders of liberty were not satisfied, and thus the original concept of federalism was modified and clarified by restricting the powers of the federal government, as well as granting them, and thus providing broad scope for judicial review of legislative acts. Little did the conservative opponents of these amendments, like Hamilton, realize how much their later partisans would depend upon what the radicals had thus added to American federalism.

The struggle for the recognition of individual rights was led by Thomas Jefferson. In his mind, the idea was linked to his general inclination to favor states' rights. This question became one of the central issues in the interpretation of the new Constitution. It was one possible view of how to interpret its provisions. Jefferson's advocacy of states' rights was embedded in a more general belief in decentralizing power as much as possible. "In government, as well as in every other business of life, it is by division and subdivision of duties alone, that all matters, great and small can be managed to perfection." Descending from the state to the county and ward, Jefferson thought of the wards as "pure and elementary republics"; a ward was a "small republic within itself," autonomous within its proper sphere. In a letter to Kercheval, July 12, 1816, he described this composite federal whole as follows: "(1) the general federal republic for all concerns, foreign and federal; (2) that of the state for what relates to its own citizens exclusively; (3) the county republics for the duties and concerns of the county; (4) the ward republics, for the small and yet numerous interesting concerns of the neighbourhood."[8] For it is in the local community that the mass of citizens can personally participate in government. It is evident that we have here a revival of notions which were first expounded by Althusius. Jefferson became the most prominent exponent of the idea that there is a line of power which marks the division between national and state governments. It makes them two "coordinate" governments, "each sovereign and independent in its own sphere." The complement to such ideas is the insistence upon a right of secession. These ideas were continually argued in the half century before the Civil War situation developed; they gave rise to such steps as the Kentucky Resolution, drafted by Jefferson, and proclaiming that "the United States of America are not united on the principle of unlimited submission to their general government" but rather that it was a compact to which "each State acceded as a State" contracting with the other States and that "as in all other cases of compact among parties having no common judge, each party has an equal right to judge for itself." They finally found their most vigorous restatement in John Calhoun's *Disquisition on Government*[9] (1851), which built on the idea of a kind of group federalism expressed in his notion of concurrent majorities, meaning that a community's will can only be ascertained by taking into account the majorities in each of its major constituent groups. The *Disquisition* called the United States a "democratic federal republic" by which Calhoun meant "a community of states, and not the government of a single state or nation." Falling back on the time-worn doctrine that sovereignty is indivisible, he claimed it for the states, which must be judges of their own power. Nullification of acts not acceptable to the people of a particular state and, eventually, secession—these were the essence of the American concept of federalism, Calhoun argued. Actually, both history and theory proved him wrong. His was a much older concept of federalism which it had been precisely the achievement of the Constitution to transcend.

The context within which such a radical reinterpretation of American federalism was espoused was, of course, the southern interest in slavery as a mainstay of its economy. The issue touched one of the fundamentals of human living together. If it is true that federalism enables people of very divergent fundamental outlooks to work together politically because it makes it possible to structure the community in accordance with these divergencies, it is nonetheless true that some disagreements on fundamentals might disrupt the federal union, and this was put, by Abraham Lincoln, into the classic short formula: "This government cannot endure permanently half slave and half free." That a resolution of the slavery question was essential to the maintenance of American federalism seems evident.

One of the most important results of the Civil War was to clear the road for the evolution of a new centralizing federalism in which the concept underwent a steady evolution toward the predominance of the nation and its government. The economic development of the vast continent into one interrelated economy, the expansion overseas in conjunction with the Spanish-American War and the consequent adaptation of constitutional tradition of Western territory to colonial dependencies, such as Puerto Rico and Hawaii, and the increasing involvement in European and world politics, to mention only the three most important elements, gave the federal or rather national government a new pre-eminence. To be sure, the states jealously guarded their ancient prerogatives, but as conditions changed, the progressive forces in the country, which once upon a time in the days of Jefferson had stood up for states' rights, increasingly turned to the national scene for the realization of their goals. Such movements as the Grange and organized labor unions might have sectional roots, but they aspired to shaping national policy, and had to, if they were to realize their goals.

This new federalism in practice was slow to express itself in theory, but when we turn to James Bryce's celebrated *The American Commonwealth,* first published in 1888,[10] we find ourselves confronted with a rather different federalism than the one which had dominated American thought before the

Civil War. Ideas such as those of Calhoun had become unthinkable. The United States is one, a commonwealth, a whole, which may suitably be described first and foremost in terms of the national government, as the first part of Bryce's study is entitled. At the outset, of course, Bryce noted what he calls a "sentimental" hesitation of the American people to call themselves a nation. He said that "America is a Commonwealth of commonwealths, a Republic of republics, a State which, while one, is nevertheless composed of other States even more essential to its existence than to theirs." Yet he observed the strong centralizing tendencies and, the explicit amendments apart, pointed to three factors as of prime importance in promoting these tendencies. First there was and is the extensive (broad) interpretation by the judiciary of the powers of the national government, second, congressional legislation impinging on state activities, third, the "exertions" of the executive power. This last factor could be put more effectively by speaking of the tremendous growth of the federal bureaucracy, from 23,000 in 1841 to 256,000 in 1901. (It has continued to grow at about the same rate, and by 1966 stood at 2,645,000.) The new federalism culminated in the rapid extension of federal activities under the presidency of Woodrow Wilson. Though schooled in the tradition of the South, Wilson was a social and economic progressive who was ready to employ the national government for broad schemes of social betterment. His administration and the ideological change which it heralded (and which was carried further by Franklin D. Roosevelt) must be seen as the triumph of the new democratic forces. It is this new democracy which has really altered the American concept of federalism. Not only the equal representation of the states in the Senate, which gives the voters of Vermont and Nevada many times the impact on national affairs that the voters of New York or California possess, but also the role of the judiciary, more especially the Supreme Court, came under continuing attack by these democratic forces. In fact, these institutions have remained part of the constitutional structure, but the democratizing of the senatorial elections, as well as certain important changes in the outlook of the Supreme Court, more especially the ever-repeated insistence upon Congress as the voice of the people have brought about dynamic, if subtle, changes. More and more, the states appear as administrative subdivisions of the nation, government survivals of another day which must be supported by grants-in-aid, supervised and coordinated by a growing federal bureaucracy,[11] retained as training and proving grounds for political leadership on the national stage.

To pick up the thread of federal theorizing outside America, we must return to the eighteenth century. In the period of American constitution-making, federal theory had a rebirth in Rousseau and Kant. Rousseau's belief in small communities as the only sound basis for democratic politics (and probably also his Swiss background) convinced him of the importance of federating such communities. More especially in his *Considerations on the Government of Poland* he favored the federal elements, embryonic though they were in Poland's traditional order.[12] Rousseau had no searching insight, however, into the real functioning of a democratic federal order. Since he rejected representation, because it was incompatible with his notion of the "general will," he had no way of structuring a federal order such as was about to be designed in America.[13] Kant, by abandoning the radically democratic tendency of Rousseau's general political outlook, made the idea of a world-wide federation of republics the basis not so much of military defense as of a world-wide political order based on law.[14] Yet, the republics composing this federal world order were unitary republics in which there was no federal principle at work. Kant, like Rousseau, did not move beyond the traditional federalism as developed by Althusius; indeed his theory was retrogressive, when compared with the American design.

Writings on federalism multiplied during the nineteenth century. Especially in America and Germany, there was a great deal of legal controversy, mostly revolving around the issue of "sovereignty" and the dichotomy of the federal state and federation of states[15]—a theoretically arid controversy of great practical importance. More interesting, and from a theoretical viewpoint more original were the views of Alexis de Tocqueville and Pierre Joseph Proudhon. The former's were essentially a commentary on the American innovations. De Tocqueville fully appreciated that they were based on a "novel" theory which he considered "a great invention" in political science. He clearly recognized the crucial point that "the subjects of the Union are not States, but private citizens" and "the Union rules individuals." In explaining this novel approach, De Tocqueville soundly appreciated that a national community had come into being along with the regional ones. Most of his thoughts had been stated quite adequately, as far as federalism is concerned, in *The Federalist,* but De Tocqueville highlighted them by persuasively contrasting America with earlier federations and by assessing fifty years of actual experience with the new scheme. He could write, a generation before the Civil War, that "the Union is as happy and free as a small people, and as glorious and as strong as a great nation."[16] Yet he misjudged the union's durability. Thinking of the peoples of the component states as nations, he "refused to believe in the duration of a government which is called upon to hold together forty different peoples." Rightly guessing that the American population would reach 150 million before another hundred years had passed, he asserted that "where there are a hundred millions of men, and forty distinct nations, unequally strong, the continuance of the federal government can only be a fortunate accident."[17] Had he understood the dynamics of the federal process better, he might have avoided the error. Basically, De Tocqueville stayed with the older theory of federalism of a Montesquieu.

This return to the older view of federalism was even more pronounced in the conception set forth by Proudhon. Bitterly opposed to Marx's centralist thinking, Proudhon revived the notion of federalism. Some of his formulations sound like translations from Althusius, more especially his emphasis on contract. Proudhon claimed that under a federal contract the contractants—the heads of families, the communes, the cantons, the provinces, and eventually the states—"not only oblige themselves bilaterally and mutually toward each other, but in concluding such a pact they also reserve to themselves more rights, more freedom, more authority, and more property than they give up."[18] For Proudhon, federalism consisted of a continuous give-and-take between inclusive community and component communities. Such organic interrelation, co-operation, and exchange is a universal principle of political organization. However, Proudhon let the higher, more inclusive community be subordinate to the lower, thereby abandoning the truly federal scheme in favor of a loose and anarchic relationship, characteristic of international relations. The contract of federation, he said, had as "its object to guarantee to the component states their sovereignty." He insisted that the competence (attributions) of the federal government could never exceed in number and substance those of the component units. There is basis in federal experience for such an assertion. It would have been approved, perhaps, by Calhoun and the makers of the Kentucky Resolution; indeed, it failed to grasp the new federal principle. Even so, Proudhon predicted that the coming century would be the century of federalism, and he was right about that.

For the twentieth century has seen great developments in federalism. In America particularly, as already noted in the previous chapter, a reinterpretation of federalism has occurred in connection with the successive phases of American expansion, both internal and external. The centralizing tendencies which industrialization fostered became more pronounced after the Civil War and culminated in Wilson's "New Freedom." Following a period of reassertion of states' rights during which conservative forces and interests shifted from federal to local support, a vigorous reassertion of governmental concern with the general welfare led to "cooperative federalism"—a design in which *both* federal and state authorities resumed a policy of extending governmental control and regulation and, in so doing, were pushed to collaborate in the execution of these policies. Finally a pattern of including in such collaboration "private" economic groups —a pattern foreshadowed in earlier agricultural extension work which had organized cooperation between federal, state, local, and farmer groups—has been hailed in the 1960's as "creative" federalism. It seeks to mobilize private interests as well as public agencies in intergovernmental programs.[19] All this can be meaningfully interpreted when the federalizing process is given central attention.

On the national, international, and local level, as well as in political group life, all kinds of federal systems have been adopted. In the course of all this activity, the former rigid patterns have been dissolving and since mid-century the former emphasis on structure and design has given way to a recognition of the federal process, as indicated in the previous chapter. These theoretical issues will be part of the analyses which follow.[20] The new stress on process has, in other words, been stimulated by the study of the social structure and forces which promote the development of a federal regime. Among these "factors" molding the federalizing of a political order, diversities in linguistic and national composition have been of prime importance. To these we shall turn in the next chapter.

NOTES TO CHAPTER 2

1. For Althusius, see my introduction to Johannes Althusius, *Politica Methodice Digesta* (1932); Otto von Gierke, *Johannes Althusius und die Entwicklung der naturrechtlichen Staatstheorien* (1880; 1929); in English as *The*

Development of Political Theory (1939). Chapter V places Althusius within the broader context of antecedent federal thought.

2. Hugo Grotius, *De Jure Belli et Pacis* (1625), Book I, chapter III, paras. 17 ff.

3. Montesquieu, *Esprit des Lois* (1748), Book IX, chapters I–III.

4. Alexander Hamilton, John Jay, and James Madison, *The Federalist—A Commentary on the Constitution of the United States,* ed. Henry Cabot Lodge (1888). See also Gottfried Dietze, *The Federalist* (1960).

5. *The Federal Convention and the Formation of the Union of the American States,* ed. Winton U. Solberg (1958), pp. 42–51. See also the introduction, pp. lxx–lxxxvii.

6. For a recent admirable analysis and description of the Convention, see Clinton Rossiter, *1787—The Grand Convention* (1966), pp. 170 ff., and throughout. For the actual record, as reconstructed, see Max Farrand, *The Records of the Federal Convention* (3 vols., 1911).

7. See note 4 above.

8. Thomas Jefferson, *The Works of Thomas Jefferson,* ed. Paul L. Ford (1905), Vol. 12, p. 9.

9. John C. Calhoun, *A Disquisition on Government* (1851), in *The Works of John C. Calhoun* (1853), Vol. I, pp. 1–107.

10. James Bryce, *The American Commonwealth* (1888; 1924), chapters II–IV.

11. J. P. Clark, *The Rise of the New Federalism: Federal-State Cooperation in the United States* (1938); Morton Grodzins, *The American System* (1966), chapters 2(IV), 12, and 16(I).

12. See on this, as well as on the related ideas of Montesquieu, the interesting essay by Stanley Hoffmann in *Area and Power,* ed. Arthur A. Mass (1959), especially pp. 113 ff. and 120 ff. Hoffmann overstresses the centralist tendency in Rousseau.

13. See on this Robert Derathé, *Le Rationalisme de Jean-Jacques Rousseau* (1948), *passim,* and Carl J. Friedrich, *Inevitable Peace* (1948), pp. 171 ff.

14. Friedrich, *op. cit.* (note 13 above), *passim* and chapter VI.

15. See on this Rupert Emerson, *State and Sovereignty in Modern Germany* (1928), chapter III.

16. Alexis de Tocqueville, *De la Démocratie en Amerique* (1835–40); in English, ed., P. Bradley (1948), chapters VII and VIII, especially pp. 171, 451–52.

17. *Ibid.,* p. 414.

18. For the quotation, see Pierre Proudhon, *Du Principe Fédératif* (1863); ed. Jean-Charles Brun, with introduction, 1921), pp. 104–5. He generalizes the civil law contract notions, and more particularly the kind of contract called *synallagmatique* (bilateral) and *communative* (mutual).

19. See on this the references given in notes 7 and 8 of the previous chapter. The term "creative federalism," employed by President Johnson since 1964, is not very accurate in describing the new trend; it is an extension of cooperative federalism in which the "sharing" that Grodzins has emphasized is *extended* to nongovernmental agencies and may therefore more suitably be dubbed "extensive federalism." See besides Scheiber's paper the many valuable publications of the Senate Subcommittee and, more particularly, of its chairman, Senator Edmund Muskie of Maine.

20. Before concluding this chapter, let me cite Sobei Mogi, *The Problem*

of *Federalism—A Study in Political Theory* (1931); Arthur E. Sutherland, *Constitutionalism in America—Origin and Development of Its Fundamental Ideas* (1965); M. J. C. Vile, *The Structure of American Federalism* (1961); and Edward McWhinney, *Comparative Federalism: States' Rights and National Power* (1962).

3

FEDERALISM AND NATIONALISM

NATIONALISM HAS PLAYED a decisive if not always helpful role in the federalizing process. The interaction of the two, both in theory and in practice, is a complex one. The powerful emotional appeal of nationalism and its crucial role in building the community basis for the modern state are universally acknowledged. Federal relationships may be utilized to provide a political order for a nation to be united out of separate and distinct entities, as was the case in Germany in the nineteenth century, that of India in the twentieth. Or federalism may serve as a means of combining several nations or nationalities into one political order, as is the case in Switzerland and Belgium, and is the hope of those who are working on the unification of Europe.

Nationalism is generally acknowledged to be probably the most potent political force of the contemporary world. There has been a good deal of discussion and argument over its nature. Nationalism, it has been said "is a state of mind," animating a national group to express itself in "what it regards as the highest form of organized activity, a sovereign state."[1] Nationalism would thus be the conscious will to give a nation a political order, to provide it with a state. Such has certainly been the nature of a great deal of nationalism since the emergence of European nations in the sixteenth century. But nationalism is not merely a state of mind, but a political movement highlighting particular aspects of group life. As a movement it creates a new kind of political community, pre-occupied with a common cultural heritage, especially in terms of language. It is therefore quite possible for two nationalisms to clash within the boundaries of a single state, and indeed for two nationalisms to overlap, as has recently happened in Canada, where the all-Canadian nationalism asserting the unity of Canada has been rivaled by the separatist nationalism of the French Canadians.

In the early stages of European nations, language played a decisive role in the shaping of national sentiment. In both Italy and Germany the first manifestations of nationalism were intimately linked to the birth of a vernacular literature such as that fashioned by Dante, Petrarch, and Boccaccio in Italy, by Luther in Germany. Nationalism and linguistic self-discovery went hand in hand. Yet, this is not a universal rule. In Switzerland nationalism transcends the linguistic boundaries of French, German, and Italian and welds a nation out of disparate linguistic groups. The same task now confronts many of the newer nations where, especially in Africa, a bilingual or multilingual composite population seeks to achieve a national consensus. This has also been the hope in Belgium, Canada, and other linguistically divided communities. The ever-present temptation of the majority (or even the largest minority) to impose its own language upon the rest of its fellow-countrymen is likely to engender a violent reaction. It has been so in Belgium, Canada, Italy (the Tyrols), and India, to mention only some striking cases (to be treated later in greater detail). Therefore, even though a nation may be constituted and defined without reference to the unity of language,[2] nationalism feeds upon the desire and need of people to communicate with each other in their "own" language.

Nor is this fact to be wondered at. The coming together of human beings into communities and the experience of self in confronting the outside world is inconceivable without communication. Even many animals have developed elaborate systems of communication. The elaboration of communication is language. In any developed sense, community means, therefore, language. To communicate by words is one of the basic traits of man.[3] Anthropologists assure us that no community of men is known which did not, does not possess "the gift of speech and a well-ordered language."[4] Language expresses feelings, thoughts, and other experiences and is thus intimately linked to the distinctive life-processes of particular groups. All language is listening as well as speaking, and language is thus embedded in culture, as culture is embedded in language. They are like Siamese twins, and the passions engendered by the will to maintain a language is the expression of a will to self-maintenance and self-determination. Federalism provides the opportunity to give maximum scope to such linguistic self-expression. Bilingual (or even multilingual) communication may be a substantial burden in official and unofficial communication, but it is the necessary price which must be paid where otherwise only an imposed single language is likely to disrupt the community and tear apart those bonds which might otherwise suffice for effective political life.

The relation of language to nationality and race has been a major weapon in the armory of modern politics, whether the argument ran toward diversity or unity. Nationalism implies a necessary and close relationship between common language and effective political community. The argument in favor of a racial basis of language and political community may be largely specious. What is not specious is that a common language and its common sayings and habits of mind and speaking is a decisive bond of all political community. Determined efforts to force the issue, such as that of "Americanizing" immigrants through the teaching of English, or of reviving ancient languages are the result of this incontrovertible fact; they have often failed. For since nationalism and linguistic self-discovery go hand in hand, such efforts may serve to reveal the lack of community, as well as stimulate resistance. Indeed, the movement that is nationalism finds many of its most potent symbols in linguistic expressions. It bears a resemblance to other symbols of exclusive group loyalty, but is distinguished from them by its concern with cultural self-identity; its most pronounced form is literary self-expression. All values and beliefs are colored by this self-identity, and there is associated with it a firm conviction that only the member of that particular national group can fully appreciate its "unique" literary creations.[5]

The disruptive potential of such linguistic identification with a literary tradition is, of course, particularly great when the group with a separate identity speaks a major language of another powerful political community.[6] This problem is pronounced in such cases as Belgium and Canada. The Royal Commission Report on Canada (1965) speaks of this aspect in measured terms: "It is probably true that the discovery by some of them [French Canadians] of a world which is French-speaking [France, Belgium, Switzerland, former French Africa, and so forth] has a reassuring effect and brings them promise of valuable cultural enrichment; in this way French Canadians are becoming more conscious of being a part of a much larger cultural world; some of them are thus having the experience of a world-wide French community."[7] The situation is further aggravated when the link is to a nation across the border, as is so common in Europe.

American experience, reinforced by German and Swiss experience, is by contrast the most telling in showing what a federal order can accomplish in facilitating the growth and the building of a nation. In sharp contrast to the forcible uniting of disparate elements by the monarchical rulers of medieval Europe, American federalism provided a chance of linking unity with diversity as the democratic alternative. Federalism thus provides the only voluntary approach to the task of coordinating disparate national elements. It is being experimented with all over the world, in India, as well as in Nigeria and the Congo, and, finally, in Europe. The issues are similar, but usually contain a specific and unique element. Thus in India, the federalizing process encompasses an entire culture, in many ways more complex than that of Europe, more diversified in religion, language, and social customs. In Nigeria, similar complexities are compounded by the absence of an overarching tradition, such as the great literature of India provides for the cultural elites in many parts of that country. The key issue is whether a national sentiment can become associated with the federal order of things.[8]

One can say that the Swiss more than any other people have succeeded in handling nationality difficulties successfully by means of a number of democratic instrumentalities, especially direct popular action through initiative and referendum. The referendum is useful in making possible an affirmation of a collective sense of belonging to a distinctive constituency, but the problem of how to define that constituency in particular circumstances belongs among the most delicate problems of political strategy.

It has been repeatedly argued that nationalism really starts in the French Revolution,[9] and that the "age of nationalism" began with this cataclysmic event. Hans Kohn has written that "nationalism as we understand it is no older than the second half of the eighteenth century," and that "its first great manifestation was the French revolution." Much depends, of course, upon what the qualification "as we understand it" is intended to connote precisely. But on the strength of Kohn's own characterization of nationalism as a certain state of mind, it would seem that it is considerably older than the eighteenth century. On the whole it seems more accurate to look upon France as a relative newcomer in the field, though undoubtedly the second half of the eighteenth century presents a culminating point of nationalism in France. Yet similar outbursts preceded that of the French, in England in the middle of the seventeenth century, and in Germany in the first quarter of the sixteenth century. A most interesting correlation of these outbursts of nationalism in conjunction with "great" revolutions and the subsequent formation of a nation was undertaken by Rosenstock-Hüssy some years ago.[10] In such a perspective, nationalism appears as a general trend in Western culture which finally was universalized in the sequel to the French and American revolutions. It has since swept the globe, and is still gaining momentum among the non-European peoples.

Is it an accident that the same epoch saw the rise and spread of modern, dynamic, constitutional federalism? Or are both movements related to the same general trends? Treading in the footsteps of Rousseau, Montesquieu, and Althusius, Proudhon stressed the small group as the essential condition of the good life. In this type of thinking there are at work elements of a religious tradition, which had expressed itself in the proliferation of sects, and at an earlier age in the establishment of religious orders and monasteries. It has been shown that these orders in their constitutions often advanced rather far toward developing federal structures,[11] providing each component group with real participation in the making of basic decisions. If nationalism is understood as *inter alia* a substitute for religion[12] and federalism may be said in a sense to be modeled on monastic precedents, then both may be seen as linked to the process of secularization. This process helped to shape the intellectual history of Europe since the Renaissance, but culminated in the French Revolution.

It was very natural that the divisive propensities of the modern age—each separately motivated and shaped by a historical evolution of its own—should have been a contributing factor in the spread of federalism, on the level of government as well as in the broad range of social and economic organizations. Each of man's basic concerns, his religion, his language, and his ideology, can and does serve in constituting subcommunities in a larger, more comprehensive community that might be based upon other values, interests, and beliefs, such as security and prosperity. Hence a federal order on whatever level would make the realization of these basic concerns possible in autonomous groups that are federally united with others of divergent view. Whether we look at Europe or India, at the United States, Switzerland, or Germany—to mention five instances of effective federalizing—religious, linguistic, and ideological (party) factors are important ingredients of their evolving federal unions. And to the extent that opposition is vital, it is well worth remembering that federalism provides opportunities for an opposition to participate in governing a political community and thereby to demonstrate its "loyalty" to the established political order, as well as its capacity to take over the government at large on the federal level. (See chapter 7.)

What all this basically leads to is the conclusion that federalism and nationalism are historically linked, because they are both also tied to the growth of democracy. Indeed, it has been asserted that nationalism was the essential condition for the democratizing of the modern state. Against such a view, it seems sounder to see democracy and nationalism in a "dialectic" relation. As one writer put it, they were "in their origin contemporary movements" and therefore many of the conditions for one also served to condition the other. But the hard core of nationalism was a need for and a belief in a particular kind of community, whereas democracy in its modern constitutional forms sprang from belief in the common man, or rather belief in man, and was fashioned to serve the needs of a free and competitive society. Democracy's drive is in the direction of an ultimate constitutional world order transcending nation, state, and sovereignty. It is therefore true to say that the link between nationalism and democracy "created an antinomy which ultimately threatened to thwart the realization of democracy" on a world-wide basis.[13] At least this is so in the European and American perspective. In the newly emerging nations any emergent world order will certainly have to be constructed from the building blocks of states and nations, rather than from the beliefs involved in constitutional democracy or, more especially, individual rights.

The dialectic of nationalism and democracy is imbedded in much modern thought typified by Rousseau, whose position calls for some further comment. As the prophet of both, he exaggerated each, and provided them with the common mystique of the "general will." Yet the general will, when operating beyond the local community, makes sense only in terms of a nation welded into complete unity by undisputed common values and beliefs held by each and all individuals— all of them *Émiles* after a thoroughgoing indoctrination. Or rather, this is true unless there is superimposed a faith in a categorical imperative shaping the will of most individual men in terms of norms of universal validity—norms discoverable in the individual's conscience. As a consequence, these norms mold the nation's state and sovereignty, founding and eventually achieving a constitutional reign of law. But, as Hegel observed in rejecting the enlightened Kantian cosmopolitanism, the nation's self in its identity and seclusion is denied by such a general imperative.[14]

Hans Kohn has written, in commenting on Rousseau, that he

taught men that their foremost loyalty was due to the "national" community, based upon law, liberty and equality, and held together by a feeling of brotherhood and mutual devotion. Such a community could only be founded on the will of all its members. To educate their will, to create conditions favorable to its formation and duration, became the central task of nation building.[15]

This was, of course, the basis of Jacobin nationalism. Yet, the Jacobins' rabid and perfervid nationalism had a universal appeal. In conquering all of Europe, Napoleon still flattered himself to be the executor of France's "civilizing mission." When Hegel thought he recognized Napoleon on his white charger as an embodiment of the world spirit, he justified such "missions" by allowing many nations in turn to become the instruments of the world spirit in its universal significance for the forward march of mankind.

To recall these familiar and by now banal formulas serves to elucidate the broader meaning of the level of political development which nation, state, and sovereignty constituted. The nation has always been one among several, a member of a "family," a state confronting other states "in the posture of a gladiator," to use Hobbes' memorable phrase. All by itself, in the lonely singularity of a Roman or a Chinese or even a medieval empire, the nation and its state as a level of political life, comprehensive and exclusive, could not exist. A boundary is of its very essence.

The problems created by the relation of federalism and nationalism are sharply defined in the efforts made during this century to bring into being some kind of federally united Europe. The most difficult issue which endangers such efforts (as can be seen, for example, in India) is whether it is possible to cultivate two rival nationalisms alongside each other. Much thought on loyalty tends to stress its exclusiveness, since divided loyalties are patent sources of conflict. And yet, human experience is familiar with divided loyalties of all kinds, in interpersonal relations of family and profession. Analogies suggest themselves which we cannot develop here, except to hint that for most men the loyalty to wife and mother have to be effectively coordinated and integrated. Under democratic conditions, unfortunately, the potential conflict situation offers a rich source for demagogic exploitation. Dr. Johnson's poignant observation that "patriotism is the last refuge of a scoundrel" has its apt relevance to the agitators for nationalist causes in the twentieth century. Federalism, by providing channels for intergroup communication, by delaying precipitate action and offering a stage for intergroup compromise, seems to be one of the political instrumentalities for negotiating the problem of a divided loyalty, by affording both integrative and differentiating forces some room to operate in.

In successful federal regimes there develops in time something that has been called the "federal spirit" or the "federal behavior." It is a highly pragmatic kind of political conduct, which avoids all insistence upon "agreement on fundamentals" and similar forms of doctrinaire rigidity. Such behavior proceeds in the spirit of compromise and accommodation. It is molded by the knowledge that there are many rooms in a house that federalism builds.

NOTES TO CHAPTER 3

1. Hans Kohn, *Nationalism* (1944), chapter 1. The peculiar nationalism that is Zionism possibly helped to shape Kohn's view; see for Zionism Ben Halpern, *The Idea of the Jewish State* (1961), Vol. 1.

2. The Institut Internationale de Philosophie Politique held a colloquium on the subject of nation and nationalism at Florence (July, 1965), of which the papers were published in *Annales de la Philosophie Politique,* ed. R. Polin (1966).

3. Friedrich, *op. cit.* (note 1, chapter 1), pp. 43 ff.

4. Edward Sapir contributed a by now famous article on the subject of language to *Encyclopedia of the Social Sciences* (1931).

5. One can hear highly intelligent persons make curious comments embodying such notions. Passages carrying such implications may be found, for example, in Oswald Spengler, *Der Untergang des Abendlandes* (1919), Vol. II, pp. 62 ff.; Hermann Keyserling, *Das Reisetagebuch eines Philosophen* (1922),

Vol. I, pp. 16 f., 244 ff., 385 ff.; Vol. II, pp. 629 f., 856 f.; Salvador de Madariaga, *Portrait of Europe* (1950), pp. 18 ff.

6. See Edward McWhinney, *Federal Constitution-Making for a Multi-National World* (1966).

7. *A Preliminary Report of the Royal Commission on Bilingualism and Biculturalism* (1965), p. 114.

8. Robert O. Tilman and Taylor Cole (eds.), *The Nigerian Political Scene* (1962).

9. Kohn, *op. cit.*, chapter 1. Contra, and in support of our view, Boyd Shafer, *Nationalism: Myth and Reality* (1955), where good evidence is presented.

10. Rosenstock-Hüssy, *Die Europäischen Revolutionen* (1931), *passim*.

11. Léo Moulin, *Le Monde Vivant des Religieux—Dominicains, Jésuites, Bénédictins* (1964), chapter IX.

12. Carlton J. H. Hayes, *Essays on Nationalism* (1926), especially chapter IV.

13. Kohn, *op. cit.*, pp. 191–92.

14. In a sense, the philosophies of Kant and Hegel spell out and in their turn pursue to the bitter end, each of them, one of the horns of the dilemma built into Rousseau's doctrine of the general will—a will at once that of a nation that knows no individuals, and that of individuals who know no nation. See Friedrich, *Inevitable Peace* (1948), chapter VI, for further elaboration.

15. Kohn, *loc. cit.*

4

FEDERALISM, SOCIALISM, AND PLANNING

THE PROBLEMS which federalism presents to socialism and planning have been at issue for many years. Classical Marxism had no use for the thought and behavior required by federalism. Nor had the more pragmatic socialism nurtured in and by utilitarianism. John Stuart Mill's *Representative Government* had little to say about it. There was only one strand of socialism which was keenly interested in the federal idea and that was the unionist (syndicalist) and anarchist version of Proudhon. (See chapter 2.) An anarchic autonomy of the component parts of a federal order was its hallmark.[1]

For modern, operative federalism, these doctrinal controversies are just distant memories. Socialism has become pragmatic as the protagonist of a welfare state which most people accept, though many with reluctance, quite a few with regret. It is characteristic as well as symptomatic for the proponents of the welfare state that socialism's old battle cry "socialization of property" has yielded to the twentieth century undertaking of planning, and, more especially, planning for full employment and against the business cycle. Both in England

and in France, socialist parties discovered upon assuming power and responsibility that relatively little was accomplished for the standard of living by "nationalizing" industry, unless it was accompanied by comprehensive planning.[2]

Such planning raises very grave problems for a democracy, and it has often been claimed that the two are completely incompatible. This view is at least in part due to the fact that over-all planning was first attempted in the Soviet Union in the early twenties of this century, as it proceeded to implement the development of a totalitarian regime (which the Soviets call "true democracy"). It has become clear in the course of more recent experience that planning may be totalitarian, but that it may also be democratic. Indeed, all democratic states are instituting planning procedures in which the objectives of such a plan are periodically reviewed by the elected representatives of the people. It is possible to describe and thereby define such planning as follows: It constitutes guidance and coordination of the community's economic activities—and more especially its investments—through an over-all program directed particularly to the use of economic resources, which is shaped in accordance with the popular preferences as these are expressed through representative bodies and within the framework of a constitution. Such an over-all program describes—in quantitative terms, wherever possible—the various measures required in guiding production and distribution over a definite planning period.

It is obvious that such planning presents difficult issues to the continued operation of a federal system. Planning will have to be undertaken not only at the federal level, but at the state level as well. These two planning levels must, at the same time, be brought into harmony with each other. It may be possible to plan at the state level in a more intensive way (as has happened, for example, in Puerto Rico) if the general goal of such planning meets with the approval of the people at large. But it would obviously be destructive of the very purpose of planning if the component units went ahead with developing plans that clashed with each other and with the federal plan as well. The shared or cooperative federalism, which has been developing in the United States and elsewhere, is based upon the fact that "most of the time under most circumstances compatibility rather than conflict of interest is characteristic."[3] This cooperative federalism provides the instrumentalities for coordinating federal and state planning. It follows the pattern of the division of functions between the two levels, arbitrary and pragmatic as this division is. There is nothing inherently unfeasible about the states planning for state functions and the federal government for federal functions. In some important fields, such as highway construction, the planning of both has had to be intermeshed. But it is equally patent that such planning within an operative federal system will lack some of the neatness and precision of planning for a unitary setup with only decentralized delegation of execution to local authorities. Yet, the pattern of delegated administration (see chapter 8) which prevails in some federal systems offers an opportunity for combining comprehensive planning with differentiated implementation by local plans. What is more, the cooperative federalism which has been growing in the United States provides beginnings of delegated administration in fields particularly in need of planning, such as the previously mentioned road construction.

There can be little question that effective dovetailing of central and local planning presupposes a democratic planning process.[4] Such a planning process is basically consistent with democratic procedures, when it is treated as similar to the budgetary process; a budget has rightly been called an elementary short-range plan. The elaboration of these procedures has helped in discovering ways of developing democratic planning. Considerable difficulties arise, however, when the realities of advanced administrative patterns are taken into account. Some tentative and fragmentary approaches to a resolution of these difficulties have been developed in the United States and in the European Economic Community (EEC); they are rapidly being expanded. In this respect, the British Commonwealth also offers a wide field for experimentation and observation.

In the more mature federal systems, cooperation has increasingly replaced the former strict separation and division of federal and local activities in the economic sphere. In the newer ones such cooperation has been constitutionally provided for, and new institutions such as economic councils have been established. While the central governments have usually led in over-all planning and economic policy, the planning work in the component units (states, provinces, and so forth) has by no means been without its limited impact; in some fields, such as agriculture and labor, it has been of primary importance. It is, of course, true that these complex federal patterns of organized cooperation occasion many difficulties and delays, but the situation in Britain illustrates the equally serious difficulties of centralized and therefore top-heavy systems. Here as elsewhere the intrinsic value of federal cooperative ways must be weighed against conflicting values of efficiency and dispatch.

Fiscal and monetary policies have in recent years become a decisive instrument in the direction of a developing economy. Hence a modern federal regime cannot avoid the task of coordinating these fields, when engaged in planning. Very serious troubles plague the older federal systems such as the United States and Switzerland, where a constitutionally sanctioned division of fiscal resources impedes, if it does not render nugatory, a coordinated fiscal policy. The Federal Republic of Germany has encountered similar problems; how they have been overcome suggests some clues as to ways of dealing with such situations. In the newer federal systems a more flexible program is usually sanctioned by the constitution. The recurring preponderance of the central government's tax resources has been limited by a system of unconditional grants, often carefully protected by constitutional or legal enactment.[5]

The objection often heard that federalism is incompatible with modern development planning and coordinated economic and fiscal policies can therefore not be admitted. Nor are there clear indications that the degree of looseness or tightness of the federal structure bears any direct relation to the degree to which economic planning may be successful. In some respects, looseness helps by providing greater planning scope to a pathfinding, progressive unit; in other respects, tightness helps, because it insures a greater degree of parallel development and basic conformity. Difficulties there are plenty, but these difficulties are inherent in the continuing extension of governmental participation in economic activities; they are as real in centralized unitary systems as in federal ones, and they may be even more serious if the social structure actually calls for a federal order. (See chapter 6.) For such an order is capable of eliciting under these conditions a great degree of cooperation and loyalty, although the risk of a *liberum veto* on the part of a single unit constitutes at times a real threat. It is, however, undeniable that the greatly expanded scope of governmental activity calls for a careful balancing of central and local concerns, and much important experience is being gathered in this field at the present time.

While planning and related welfare state activities are going forward steadily, socialism in the narrower sense of the collectivization of property has been losing ground in spite of the fact that it presents fewer problems to a federal order. Such collectivization can without much difficulty be carried through in local subdivisions, as indeed it has been in the United States, in spite of fairly general hostility toward the ideology of socialism. Switzerland and Canada, to mention two other federal systems, have also seen considerable variations in the degree of collectivization in their cantons and provinces respectively. It just does not seem to matter a great deal any more; the greater chances for bureaucratic inefficiency, if not corruption, to creep into collective enterprises have dampened the ardor of former protagonists of socialism.

Notes to Chapter 4

1. Guy Héraud, *L'Europe des Ethnies* (1963), has argued that the ethnic groupings should become the basis of a future European federal order, rather than the existing states. See chapter 23 of the present work for more detail.

2. See my *Constitutional Government and Democracy* (4th ed., 1968), chapter XXIII. Although "nationalization" and "socialization" are often used interchangeably, the former is strictly speaking a special case of the latter, which may also mean the transfer to other collectivities than the nation.

3. Morton A. Grodzins, "The American Federal System," in *A Nation of States,* ed. Robert A. Goldwin (1961), p. 23. See also the same author's (with Jacob Cohen), "How Much Economic Sharing in American Federalism?," *The American Political Science Review,* Vol. LVII (1963), pp. 5–23, concluding "the two planes of government in the federal system do not pursue fundamentally antagonistic economic policies."

4. For the problem of democratic planning, see my *op. cit.* (note 2, above), chapter XXIII.

5. R. L. Watts, "Recent Trends in Federal Economic Policy and Finance in the Commonwealth," *Public Policy,* Vol. XIV (1965), pp. 380–402.

5

FEDERALISM AND
PARTY SYSTEM

THE RELATION between federalism and party structure presents
highly significant issues which have been receiving increasing
attention in recent years. The comparative analysis of party
systems has highlighted the fact that in federal regimes parties
tend toward paralleling the governmental setup. American
parties are seen essentially as federations of state parties; similar trends may be observed in other federally organized
countries. Political science has recognized for some time that
the organizational structure of parties tends to correspond to
the governmental pattern under constitutional democracy.
This is only natural, since it is one of the purposes of parties
to gain control of the government; therefore, if the government is federally structured, parties must adapt themselves to
such a structure. In Germany and Switzerland there is
stronger cohesion in the national party organizations than in
the United States, corresponding to the tighter federalism in
these countries. But the *Länder* and *Kanton* parties display a
much greater degree of autonomy than do party subdivisions
in unitary states such as England.

Before we explore these issues in somewhat greater detail, it is worth noting that the interaction between governmental structure and party organization is also to be observed in authoritarian regimes based upon a single party, except that in such systems it is the government which responds to the centralizing impact of the party. Notably in the Soviet Union the formal federalism of the governmental structure is superseded and transcended by the integrating force of the CPSU. This does not mean, as is often asserted, that the federal system has no significance in the Soviet Union; it is, as indicated before, a formalized system of decentralization. But it cannot resist the centralizing impact of the single party. For this to happen there would have to be at least two parties, so that in some of the component units the "other party" than the one in power at the center could render effective the local autonomy under some such slogan as states' rights. Even so, deep-rooted local differentiation may reinforce the local party organization, as was the case, for example, in the Ukraine and in Georgia, both of which have long traditions of resistance to central Russian predominance.[1]

The real issue, both theoretical and practical, is to evaluate such a federal party setup in comparing it with a unitary one. Parties have in many ways become the mainstay of modern democratic government and political science has come to speak of the "party state" as a distinctive form of contemporary democracy.[2] While the constitutions of the eighteenth and nineteenth centuries did not recognize parties at all, recent constitutions contain specific provisions concerning parties, notably the Basic Law of the Federal Republic of Germany.[3] But even where the constitution does not recognize parties, they have become the subject of judicial concern, notably of late in the United States, where such questions as the outlawry of subversive parties and redistricting have high-lighted the increasing importance of parties for the very functioning of democracy. The totalitarian regimes too have found it appropriate to incorporate provisions on the role and functioning of parties in their "constitutions."

In the field of European unification—a key case of progressive federalism—parties have also been of some importance. In the European assemblies, party caucuses have been developing between representatives of parties from different countries, sharing similar programs and ideologies, such as between socialist parties or between liberal parties.[4] Such efforts at effective cooperation have been important pathfinders in developing support for federal relations and a particularly interesting example can be found in the Puerto Rican parties (the Independentistas, of course, excepted), which have sought and found links with those American parties on the mainland they consider close to their own position. Any developing federal relationship is bound to seek expression in a corresponding party bond.

But there is another force which increasingly shapes the interaction between government and party and transforms the federal system through its impact on party; this is the policy aspect. We have encountered this force already in the discussion of planning; yet, not only in the economic planning sphere, but even more insistently in the sphere of foreign and defense policy is it to be felt. There is increasing need for a fully integrated national policy and this need has been taken care of primarily by party effort. It is, to speak of the United States, simply not true that only presidential elections help to federate local parties into a national body; the need for an integrated foreign and defense policy has become an additional and ever-present factor, as contrasted with the intermittent presidential elections. The creation of national policy committees which occurred in the 1950's is expressive of this trend. Even the much sloganized "bi-partisan foreign policy" has its role to play in this syndrome of interacting factors, although it clashes with the tradition of two party politics in countries like the United States. For a policy field that must ever seek to transcend party controversy surely involves federal integration. Therefore, this universal trend, manifested in Europe in the insistent demands for an effective coordination of foreign policy, makes any plan illusory which presupposes a distinctive foreign and defense policy for a member state, even if it is merely an associated state of a federal system. What it does call for is adequate procedures of consultation and participation in decision-making which will render such integrated policy fully "democratic."[5]

The inner divisions within parties, when reinforced by local issues, make the difficulties of effectuating such central coordination formidable indeed. In the United States, both parties contain an internationalist and a nationalist (isolationist) wing which can by no means be identified with the progressive and conservative wings in both parties. Comparably, in the Federal Republic of Germany, all three parties contain elements that differ sharply on such crucial matters as European unification, cooperation with France, and the Cold War. A local leader may be an exponent of a divergent policy position, to which his federally reinforced party position may enable him to give additional weight. Switzerland has always been troubled in maintaining its traditional neutrality when the sympathies of French-speaking, German-speaking, and Italian-speaking Switzerland become entangled in the rivalries of the neighboring great states. It is one of the marvels of Swiss federalism that she has been recurrently able to overcome these internal tensions through the deep loyalty of all Swiss for their traditional order. In cases such as Belgium and Canada, the parties have had to respond to divergent national sentiments, possibly aggravated by foreign policy issues. Belgian conservative elements of the Flemish persuasion have traditionally leaned toward Germany, even to the point of imperiling the national foreign policy. French Canadian sentiment, though by no means favorable toward "laicist" and "godless" France, has been hostile toward a vigorous maintenance of a foreign policy of close cooperation in the British Commonwealth of Nations and is becoming more radical in this respect. Under such circumstances, parties may have to provide the real battlefield for the reintegration of policy when the formal federal arrangements foster division and disunity. It has been rightly observed that there has been a tendency to treat as cause and effect this interrelation between party and constitutional structure, when it is actually a matter of circular interaction.[6] It is therefore right to conclude that

> . . . in a federal system decentralization and lack of cohesion in the party system are based on the structural fact of federalism, but . . . the degree to which these become the dominant characteristics of the distribution of power within the political parties is a function of a variety of other governmental and social factors which are independent of the federal structure or are merely supportive of its tendencies.[7]

It is therefore necessary to turn to the exploration of some of these "other social factors" which constitute the social substructure of a federal system.

Notes to Chapter 5

1. Klaus von Beyme, "Federal Theory and Party Reality in the Soviet Union," *Public Policy,* Vol. XIII (1964), pp. 395–412.

2. Gerhardt Leibholz, *Politics and Law* (1965), pp. 37 ff., and his *Strukturprobleme der Modernen Demokratie* (1958; 1964), where the same issue is treated at greater length.

3. Notably Article 23 of the Basic Law; there are similar provisions to be found in the Soviet, Yugoslav, and related constitutions.

4. Ernst B. Haas, *The Uniting of Europe—Political, Social, and Economic Forces, 1950–1957* (1958), especially chapter 11.

5. *Ibid.*

6. David B. Truman, "Federalism and the Party System," in *Federalism Mature and Emergent,* ed. Arthur W. MacMahon (1955), pp. 115 ff.; and William H. Riker, *Federalism* (1964), p. 101.

7. Truman, *op. cit.* (note 6 above), p. 133.

6

FEDERALISM AND
SOCIAL STRUCTURE

THE DISCUSSION OF FEDERALISM in relation to party structure cannot be carried through without giving more detailed consideration to the issues raised by the social structure of the political community concerned. The conflict of nationalities is only one of several aspects and perhaps in an era of worldwide social struggles not even the most urgent one. Federalism has been praised as providing an opportunity for experimentation in a more limited area—that is, for testing out possible solutions to urgent problems. But it has also been criticized and even denounced as providing a refuge for backward elements, for resisting effective social change. The history of every federal system is replete with illustrations supporting both contentions; for they are both true and indeed are merely the concrete manifestation for that organized diversity and multiformity which is the very reason for federal arrangements. Obviously, the looser the federal bond, the greater will be the potential diversity; consequently both praise and blame will increase.

It is very natural that the divisive propensities in the contemporary world and the universal trend toward pluralism in combination with economic pressures, reinforced by military necessities, for ever larger units of effective cooperation should have provided the main support for the forward march of federalism. For since each basic human concern—a man's religion, his language, his ideology, and so forth—serves to form subcommunities within a larger, more comprehensive community (or sustains them, if a larger one is formed), a federal order is the only way to protect such autonomous self-realization in combination with others holding divergent views. Among the current issues there is found, therefore, a marked tendency to pay increasing attention to the patterning of the social substructure of federal orders,[1] to explore with all the more advanced techniques of quantitative analysis the kind of community which a particular political order is intended to serve,[2] and to determine by ever more refined and sophisticated indices the extent, the depth, and the vitality of differentiations in communal life which might deserve constitutionally protected autonomy.[3]

One of the most telling illustrations of the relevance of social structure to the functioning of federalism is, of course, the issue of race relations in the United States. But it is hardly necessary to describe this situation in all its complexity.[4] It is as well to realize that it is in no sense unique in the recent politics of federal orders; rather, it is an instance of a recurrent pattern of federal problems. One important aspect of the social substructure is its role in remolding federal relations. Puerto Rico is an illustration in point. Just as in Puerto Rico the transformation of the island into an industrial community has significantly altered the issues and trends of Puerto Rican federal relations, so it is generally true that social substructure provides the dynamic processes which cause a general transformation of a federal system. In a sense, the history of the United States is an imposing demonstration of this general proposition. The probable amazement of the makers of the American Constitution if they were able to observe what has become of their work has often been commented upon, and slogans such as that about the horse-and-buggy age have highlighted the point. Yet it all becomes quite understandable once the social substructure and its transformations are taken into account. The rival forces of integration and differentiation are continually at work to alter the pattern of values, interests, and beliefs which shapes the social structure. The study of social structure in relation to federalism has, therefore, helped us to understand better the dynamic nature of federal orders, to look upon a federal system as subject to continual change, rather than as a static design fixed forever in an immutable distribution of functions.[5] As suggested before, this dynamic aspect of federalism is seen when it is understood as giving rise to a federalizing process.

In a way, this is a very old argument. When, prior to its adoption, the American Constitution was debated, in 1787 and 1788, the regional differences were a significant factor. Indeed, quite a few observers believed that no real unity could ever be achieved. Thus Chateaubriand wrote in his *Memoirs:*

> It is immensely difficult to create a country out of states without any community of religion and interests, states which have been peopled by different stocks and are living on varied soils and under diverse climates. . . . How many centuries will be needed to make these elements homogeneous?[6]

Similar arguments were brought forward in justifying or opposing federalism in Germany, India, and elsewhere; it is a key argument in conjunction with the extended discussion concerning European unification. Most of these arguments are rather general, however, and the very fact that they can be and have been applied on both sides of the question demonstrates their imprecision. Is it, then, possible to determine a definite and meaningful correlation between the quantitatively described balance of differentiations and integrating factors and the suitability and workability of federal relations? It has recently been affirmed, but the evidence is, so far, inconclusive.[7] Generally speaking, the social structure of a country like Britain is as pluralistically diversified as that of Germany, and more so than perhaps Australia or Canada. It is more diversified, probably, than that of Switzerland, except for language.

Leaving aside the nationality aspects of social structure, dealt with above (chapter 4), there are three other components which are of primary importance in determining it—religion, economic activity (including urbanization), and class structure. There may also be special features, such as the caste system of India, which further complicate the analysis. If a particular national community is regionally differentiated according to a reasonably defined distribution of adherents of different religions, a federal organization will considerably aid in negotiating bargains on issues involving the several belief systems. It may, of course, harden the conflict situations under certain circumstances, but this danger can be minimized if the political subunits do not coincide with the religious divisions, as logic might suggest, but rather divide the territory in which one religion prevails into several component units so that on its fringes subunits with mixed religious backgrounds may exist. The most striking case of this type of arrangement is Switzerland, but Germany also ranges from predominantly Catholic to predominantly Protestant subunits, so that bargaining can proceed on a variegated basis of coalition and compromise. (See chapters 17 and 20.) It is noteworthy that England, France, and Spain, three unitary states, are characterized by religious homogeneity, brought about by considerable oppression at an earlier stage of history.

In many ways, economic activity is, in the twentieth century, more important than religion. Consequently, the divisions which it produces have a significant impact upon the development of federal and regional relations. Of particular importance is the difference between agricultural and industrial interests. Where these follow a regionalized pattern, as they are likely to do, they may shape the federal relationship. Again, it could be said on available evidence that a federal organization will considerably aid in the protection of the agricultural minority—for it is agriculture which is apt to be the minority interest in modern economies. In underdeveloped countries, the reverse is likely to be the case of course, but the same principle applies in reverse. Because of this protection of the minority, bargains will in the end be more feasible, although in this instance too there is the danger that entrenched special interests will exploit and abuse the protection which federalism provides. Again, this danger can be minimized if the political subunits do not coincide with the economic divisions, but divide the territory in which, say, the agricultural interest predominates into several subunits, with some subunits containing a more or less balanced mixture of agriculture and industry. Virtually all existing federal states correspond to this pattern, though in varying degrees. In the extended discussions carried on in Germany, during the period of military government, over the question of the optimal size of component units of a future German democracy, these considerations constituted an important ingredient.[8]

It has been alleged recently that "in pure theory . . . what one ought to abrogate for federalism is a system of minority decision that imposes high external costs on everybody other than the minority."[9] But, as the author of this statement sagely remarks, the costs of such an arrangement may be too high, especially if the minority has intense feelings on the issue involved. This is true enough, but the pure theory itself may be questioned. Rarely can there be maintained such minority prevalence over any length of time. The author gives it verisimilitude by asserting that certain particular minorities are the recurrent beneficiaries of federal protection, and he prejudices the analysis by such terms as "capitalists," "landlords," and "racists." But the beneficiaries may be peasants, as well as "landlords," workers in particular industries as well as their masters, and so forth. All this goes to show that social structure provides a key to some of the most dynamic aspects of federalism. Its continual change, not necessarily caused by the federal system itself, provides much of the impetus for changes in federal relationships, be they engendered by mere convention and usage or by formal amendment.

NOTES TO CHAPTER 6

1. It is, however, characteristic that so basic a work as Talcott Parsons, *The Social System* (1951), contains no discussion of federalism. However, the literature cited below in the chapters dealing with particular countries is full of it; for example, Denis de Rougemont, *La Suisse—ou L'Histoire d'un Peuple Heureux* (1965).

2. See the work of Karl Deutsch, more especially his studies with Dr. Weilenmann on Switzerland (the major work is still to appear); and Karl Deutsch, Lewis J. Edinger, Roy C. Macridis, and Richard L. Merritt, *France, Germany and the Western Alliance—A Study of Elite Attitudes on European Integration and World Politics* (1967), which went astray, however, because of some dubious assumptions concerning social structure. See for a critical assessment Ronald Englehart, "An End to European Integration?," *The American Political Science Review*, Vol. LXI (1967), pp. 91 ff.

3. See my *Constitutional Government and Democracy* (4th ed., 1968), chapter XI.

4. Gunnar Myrdal, *An American Dilemma* (1944).

5. Morton Grodzins, *The American System* (1967), chapters 3–5. Grodzins introduced in this connection the useful category of "sharing" as a distinctive feature of modern federalism.

6. Chateaubriand, *Memoires d'Outre Tombe*, chapter 1.

7. Peter Merkl, "Federalism and Community Structure," a paper read before the Sixth World Congress of IPSA (Geneva Congress), 1964; see also Riker, *op. cit.* (note 6, chapter 5), who stresses the bargain aspect, pp. 12–16, 20–25, and 92–97; it is a new word for the old compact theory of federalism.

8. For general background, see Peter Merkl, *The Origin of the West German Republic* (1963). For the specific issue, see J. F. J. Gillen, *State and Local Government in West Germany* (1945–1953), Historical Division of the High Commission (1954).

9. Riker, *op. cit.*, p. 155; the table given there is highly questionable, both in terms of the factual basis and the implications; it is unrealistic.

7

FEDERALISM AND OPPOSITION[1]

IN GENERAL DISCUSSIONS about opposition in democratic political systems, such as the thoughtful reflections of Robert A. Dahl,[2] the role which federalism may play in providing an opposition with opportunities to oppose is often forgotten. This is curious, but perhaps in part at least the result of the fact that the institutionalization of opposition has gone farthest in Great Britain—a nonfederal state. Yet, in a sense, federalism may be looked upon as a method for institutionalizing opposition alternative to the British parliamentary system.

I propose to look upon opposition as, on the one hand, a group of persons effectively organized for the purpose of opposing the activities and policies of the government in power and, on the other, the complex of activities in which such persons might engage including their thoughts, their ideology. For the term opposition, like so many political terms, has both a personal and an operational dimension. That is to say, I propose to proceed on the assumption that it is meaningful to speak of "making opposition" as well as of "being in opposition." It is fairly evident, and may indeed be axiomatic, that the more divided the power of government, the greater the opportunities for an opposition. In a way, the careful protective devices of the British parliamentary scheme are needed, if an opposition is to have a chance, precisely because governmental power in Britain is so highly concentrated.

If we assume that, in judging federalism's operation as a pattern of opposition, we might employ certain criteria suitable for determining whether a political system increases the chances for the realization of constitutional democracy, we can state the following hypotheses: Federalism (1) increases the opportunities for dissenting minorities to make their views known to other citizens and policy-makers; (2) multiplies the opportunities for citizens to participate in political life; (3) enhances consensus in political discussion, in the sense that solutions are sought that will reduce the size, resentments, and coercion of defeated minorities, as well as of permanent minorities which cannot hope to become majorities; (4) greatly improves the chances of the peaceful resolution of conflicts; (5) aids the solving of urgent policy questions by providing an opportunity for experimenting with solutions on a limited scale; and (6) enhances confidence in, and loyalty to, a constitutional polity.[3] On the other hand, it appears doubtful whether federalism reduces "political violence," but does opposition necessarily do so? The empirical evidence is contradictory. Federalism also would appear to increase rather than decrease the chances that policy decisions are, in fact, made by minorities, rather than majorities of citizens, voters, and elected officials, although this is not necessarily so. Whether the rationality of political discussion and decision-making is greater or not, seems even more difficult to determine; sometimes it would seem to be so, at other times not. But the validity of this criterion appears in any case rather dubious, considering the uncertainty as to what is rational;[4]

and is it correct to say that a system is more democratic when it is more rational? If, then, these issues are left aside, we may examine each of the others in turn, in an effort to assess the value of federalism as a pattern for broadening the opposition's role.

Since it is of the essence of federalism to institutionalize diversity, it goes without saying, or at any rate does not require elaborate proof, that it provides increased opportunities for dissenting minorities to make their views known. Hence, dissenting minorities usually favor federalism as a means for protecting their identity. Sometimes the demonstration of this aspect takes dramatic form, as in Belgium where one part of the people, the Flemings, demanded a federal union as long as they were in the minority, while the other, the Walloons, demand it today, after having lost their majority status. Such opposition may, of course, be fragmented by federalism, as when the French-speaking Canadians are scattered all over the provinces, except for Quebec where they possess a solid majority. Even scattered they may become a highly significant factor in becoming the "little tongue on the scale," as is the case today of the Negroes in quite a few American constituencies. These and other like cases make it necessary, however, to distinguish between permanent and temporary oppositions. Elements of the population whose values, interests, and beliefs deviate markedly from the majority, because they constitute religious or cultural minorities, may provide an opposition which is static in terms of their particular concerns. This need not be so, and skillful party strategy will seek to overcome the sense of separateness of such groups, trying to integrate them into the population at large, first by attaching them to an opposition party and eventually by letting them share in the government. The Welsh provide a fair example of such a process. Federalism is likely to impede this process of integration, especially if the minority elements are concentrated in one or two of the units composing the federal union. It depends a good deal upon how the federal order is structured; if it contains adequate integrative devices this disadvantage may be kept at a minimum.

It is hard to draw the balance between the advantages and disadvantages of federalism under such conditions. The Canadian case certainly suggests the very real danger that a cultural and religious minority, in defending itself through its domination in one or more units of the union, becomes stratified in its oppositional role and eventually seeks the union's destruction through the demand for secession. But a supple handling of federal relations may in fact alleviate the tensions and provide an outlet for the minority's energy and need of cultural autonomy. The majority of the people of Puerto Rico, which constitutes a cultural minority within the United States of high self-consciousness as exemplified in its attachment to *Hispanidad,* chose to have Puerto Rico become an associated state rather than to have her seek full statehood within the American union. Such a solution to their federal relations enabled the Puerto Ricans to retain greater autonomy in exchange for lesser participation in the union's affairs.[5] These two North American examples, Canada and Puerto Rico, show that permanent opposition is both neutralized and channeled through a federal structuring of the political order.

The more interesting problems, at least from the viewpoint of the working of opposition, are presented by temporary opposition. By temporary opposition I mean an opposition which on the personal side is carried forward by men who consider themselves an integral part of the general constituency and therefore expect to become the government, that is, to convert their minority following into a majority. On the impersonal side, it is an opposition whose values, interests, and beliefs may well become those of the majority of the population. Both these aspects result in such an opposition being dynamic, rather than static; in opposing it strives to change the political situation so as to enable it to govern rather than oppose. A dynamic opposition will therefore marshal all the resources of persuasion and propaganda for the achievement of its central goal. A federal system greatly enhances its chance of doing so. For by becoming first the government in one state, *Land,* or canton, it achieves the authority and secures for itself the resources and tactical advantages which a government naturally possesses. Party history in the United States provides many interesting examples for this federally conditioned rise of oppositional elements, especially *within* parties. The radical progressivism of midwestern Republicanism in the era of Senator La Follette is of course the most striking illustration, but the so-called Bull Moose movement of Theodore Roosevelt is another one. And who would deny that the New Deal of Franklin Delano Roosevelt had its experimental beginnings in his governorship of New York State? The dangerous potential of this kind of local experimentation lies in the opportunities a federal order provides for destructive movements of opposition to install themselves and thus achieve an operating base. Here the most famous—or should we say infamous?—instance is provided by the history of the National Socialist movement. The conquest of Thuringia and other small *Länder* gave the Hitler movement the chance to "prove" its capacity to participate in German government.[6] It is, however, possible that in mature democratic societies, this danger could be minimized by providing, as does the American Constitution (Article IV, 4) and the Basic Law of the Federal Republic of Germany (Article 28, [1][3]), that the component units must maintain a constitutional democratic order. Thus opposition would be restricted to parties and formations that do not attack the basic principles of the popular consensus.[7]

A particular aspect of opposition in federal regimes is presented by the arrangements made for representation of the component units in the process of federal legislation and decision-making. The freedom of debate in the U.S. Senate, traceable at least in part to the original purpose of enhancing the deliberative scope of that (then) small group, has continually enabled a relatively small opposition in the South to delay if not prevent the adoption of effective federal legislation for racial equality. This has misled certain writers into overstating the point; in a recent study we read: "The main theoretical argument in favor of abrogating the federal guarantees to constituent units [is that]: Decisions made by constituent units are *invariably* minority decisions that impose high external costs on the national majority."[8] They are of course by no means *invariably* minority decisions, though they may be; and even if they are, they may well be those of an emergent majority which in such opposition develops its position by combating the national majority. Thus the Social Democratic Party in Germany has been enabled, because it is the governing party in a number of key *Länder* of the Federal Republic (Berlin, Hamburg, Hesse, to mention only the most important), to show its capacity for effective government through the progressive achievements of these particular *Länder* and even, in several of these *Länder,* by its ability to form viable coalitions with either of the other parties. These cases are particularly interesting, because they were accompanied by a slow but steady rise in the party's national support. Starting after the founding of the republic with less than 30 per cent, it has now risen to well over 40 per cent and is quite possibly going to outdistance the ruling party. Similar experiences have been made in Canada, where the Liberals and Conservatives have been reinforced in their oppositional roles by their ability to continue governing some province or other even while defeated on the national plane. The same holds good for Australia.[9]

A similar process seems to be shaping up in India, and it promises to break the long predominance of the Congress Party. Since the 1967 general election, opposition governments have been formed in eight of the sixteen states. At the same time, the majority of the Congress Party in the national parliament has been sharply reduced. Informed observers have reported "a general sense of relief and rejuvenation," and have insisted that the Congress Party's "long standing status as the predominant party is at an end."[10] There may follow a considerable loosening of India's federalism, with India's Communists playing an increasing role. The linguistic problem is of crucial importance,[11] but regional forces are the decisive factor. Federalism has been instrumental in shaping Indian politics, enabling this vast and complex cultural entity "to keep discourse open, to diminish fanaticism, and to facilitate the search for broadly acceptable solutions."[12]

If one considers now the specific form available to the opposition for the exercise of its oppositional capacities on the federal level, it is evident that situations may arise in which the opposition party may secure a majority in a majority of component units and thereby be enabled to make its opposition more effective. A special case is provided by the qualified majorities usually required for constitutional amendments. Switzerland has had some dramatic experiences in this connection, especially in the field of foreign affairs. Her entry into the League of Nations eventually turned upon its advocates winning sufficient support in some of the small rural cantons. Therefore, a veritable avalanche of potent national figures in politics and university life was unloosed upon the electorate to debate the issue. Similarly, since the re-establishment of the armed forces in Germany's Federal Republic required constitutional amendments, it enabled the oppositional Social Democrats, who controlled enough votes in both houses, to exact important concessions. In the case of the Federal Republic, it is generally true to say that the federal government must be closely concerned with the elections in the several *Länder*, especially when the balance in the Federal Council is a close one. For the winning or losing of a *Land* election may vitally affect the government's entire legislative program and general policy.[13]

For a full appreciation of the problem, it is necessary to consider the composition of the federal house in the national legislature. There are two primary forms: the senatorial and the council type. In the typical example of the former, the component units are represented by an equal number of representatives for each unit, who are directly or indirectly elected for a fixed term. In the council type, the units are represented through their governments, often on a weighted basis. It is this system which the Federal Republic has retained (it existed in the old Reich and under the Weimar Republic). In such an institution, the vote of each unit is cast *en bloc* and under instruction from the local government. The greater rigidity is compensated for by informal proceedings, mostly in committee, and by the close link with the federal and the *Land* bureaucracy. For the Federal Council is not really a parliamentary body, but rather a coordinator of administrative bodies. Indeed it was originally suggested by this need of integrating existing bureaucracies. The Federal Council must be seen against the background of a system of delegated administration under which the component units carry through and administer much federal legislation. (See chapter 8.) In the Federal Council, members of the opposition who also happen to occupy the higher "political" posts in the *Land* or cantonal administration are capable of participating in the shaping of federal legislation and thus of making the opposition effective in the loopholes created by holding national office. The resolution of conflict is thereby greatly aided.[14]

Special problems arise, if the confrontation of government and opposition involves the federal relationship, as was, for example, the case in Germany in the controversy over a federal television station. Even so powerful a man as Adenauer found himself abandoned by his own party's local leaders.

The issue is not a new one, but has played a significant role in the politics of federal regimes for many years. The epochal conflict between "Federalists" and "Republicans" in the early decades of the American Republic raised the problem in an acute form. Such strong presidents as Jefferson and Jackson, while committed to the doctrine of states' rights, actually expanded federal jurisdiction and were also quite effective protagonists of the prerogatives of the presidential office.

From all that has been said it ought to be clear that when federalism is understood as a process, and the role of the "federalizer" is therefore recognized, the opposition (in both senses) often operates as the federalizer and it does so in either the centralizing or the decentralizing direction. The reason is not far to seek. Since the federal structure provides for a considerable dispersion and division of power, its diverse opportunities will be exploited by any opposition. In consequence, we may be justified in formulating the proposition that a functioning and organized political opposition is a highly important and perhaps vital ingredient of constitutional federalism. By exploiting the various nooks and crannies of a federal regime, a political opposition forces the government to do the same and thereby more or less effectively contravenes any tendency on the part of the ruling party to corrode and undermine the complex structure of a federal system. This is, of course, as true of permanent as of temporary (political) oppositions. Indeed such issues as, for instance, religion, while providing a prime argument for federalism in the first place, may serve to give a federal dispersion of governmental power recurrent boosts when it comes to the fore and highlights the potentialities for protecting a permanent oppositional minority at least in its strongholds.

The obverse of this coin is that any theory of political opposition would be incomplete without due acknowledgement that federalism provides an institutionalization for the deployment of political opposition which actually works. This applies even to one-party states in which any other framework for an opposition is lacking. In the heyday of the extreme totalitarianism of Stalin and Hitler, the remnants of a federal tradition in Germany and the formal recognition of federalism in the Soviet Union served to provide some minimal protection for oppositional elements. It was not much, and the rigorous centralist control of the single party prevented it from becoming effective. In free democratic federal regimes, on the contrary, the opportunities which federalism offers to the opposition engender a federalization of the parties themselves, and even a multiplication of intraparty opposition, as we have seen. This process may go to the point where such opposition amounts to a serious threat to the party's leadership. Where the federal tradition is strong, national parties operate as federations of local parties. This is generally held to be the situation in the United States, approved by some, hotly criticized by others, but in any case causing a rather complex party pattern. Both Republicans and Democrats are divided along regional lines, among which the division between South and North is the most important.[15] But there have developed two other persistent divisions which, at crucial stages in the legislative and policy-making process, occasion a regrouping of the parties: a bipartisan internationalist grouping fights a bipartisan nationalist (formerly isolationist) one, and, similarly, the progressives in both parties—often referred to as "liberals"—combat the conservatives in both. As a consequence the pattern of opposition in the United States (and similar developments are observable in other federal systems, for example, Germany, Switzerland, India) is highly dynamic and kaleidoscopic in its shifts and realignments.

In summary, the evidence supports the hypothesis that federalism and opposition mutually strengthen and support each other, and that, more particularly, a federal regime without an operative political opposition on both the national and local level is apt to remain "on paper." At the same time, the evidence also suggests that a federal system diversifies the opposition's roles and thereby produces the danger of reducing the effectiveness of its impact upon major issues of national policy. This need not be so, but the danger exists. What is of primary significance is federalism's ability to provide a measure of institutionalization for an opposition in countries where the operation of the British model of parliamentary democracy is, for various reasons, unworkable. For it makes greater allowance for the diversity of groupings in the electorate, which would interfere with the effectiveness of an opposition in its role of opposing a centralized government.

NOTES TO CHAPTER 7

1. A substantial part of this chapter first appeared in my "Federalism and Opposition," in *Government and Opposition* (1966), Vol. I, pp. 286 ff.

2. See *Political Oppositions in Western Democracies,* ed. R. A. Dahl (1966), chapters 11–13, especially pp. 332 ff. Of the eight standards he outlines on p. 7 as measuring rods for determining whether a particular system of opposition "maximizes" the effective chances of realizing democratic goals or values, six at least seem to suggest an affirmative answer when federalism is concerned.

3. It will be noted that this set of propositions follows, with some rather significant variations, the statement in Dahl, *loc. cit.* It does not seem empirically sound to speak of "maximizing" the phenomena cited, since it is unknown what the "maximum" would be. On the subject of minimal and maximal solutions see my *Man and His Government* (1963), pp. 663 f. and *passim.*

4. See on this vexed issue the several papers in *Nomos,* VII ("Rational Decision"), including my own paper on the historical dimension.

5. Robert J. Hunter, "Historical Survey of the Puerto Rico Status Question, 1898–1965," *Status of Puerto Rico, Selected Background Studies* (U.S./Puerto Rico Status Commission: 1966), pp. 50–145, with extensive bibliography. See also Whitney T. Perkins, "The United States and the Dilemma of Political Control," *ibid.,* pp. 435–70.

6. A special feature was the chance it offered the Nazis to naturalize Hitler; without that he could not have become chancellor.

7. This problem is, of course, not peculiar to federal regimes, but is ubiquitous in contemporary society. For the underlying theoretical and philosophical issues, see my *Constitutional Reason of State* (1957).

8. William H. Riker, *Federalism* (1964), p. 151. (Italics mine.) See also p. 144: "But when national uniformity is worth more than confusion, then federalism is an impediment to freedom because it deprives the na-

tional majority of the chance to eliminate the excess costs of confusion."
The author seems to be unaware that this argument is practically identical
with one advanced by partisans of the one-party state against the confusion
and cost caused by opposition in general.

9. See for these countries the rich bibliographical material contained in
Federalism in the Commonwealth, ed. William S. Livingston (1963), and K. C.
Wheare, *Federal Government* (1946; 3d ed., 1953). For the Federal Republic
of Germany, see especially Karl-Heinz Neunreither, *Der Bundesrat zwischen
Politik und Verwaltung* (1959).

10. See Lloyd I. Rudolph and Susanne Hoeber Rudolph, "New Era for
India—Politics after the 1967 Election," *Bulletin of Atomic Scientists,*
February, 1968, p. 1.

11. W. H. Morris-Jones, "Language and Region Within the Indian Union,"
in *India and Ceylon: Unity in Diversity,* ed. Philip Mason (1967).

12. Rudolph, *op. cit.,* p. 19.

13. Such a situation confronted the German federal government in 1965–66
with regard to the election in Rhineland-Westphalia. A good deal of criticism is at times expressed in Germany over this "alienation" of the *Land*
elections, as *Land* issues are relegated to the background in favor of national
concerns.

14. Neunreither, *op. cit.,* pp. 55 ff. and 92 ff., at least as far as the more
technical and detailed aspects of controversial national legislation are concerned. In short, the involvement of a federal government in the politics
of its component units is an inevitable result of the interweaving of the
policies of the two levels, especially when the balance of the federal representative body is affected. At times such federal interference may, however,
boomerang, especially where the sense of local pride and autonomy is
strongly developed. Even so powerful a political leader as Franklin D. Roosevelt discovered, when he tried to interfere with the re-election of some
conservative Southern senators who had opposed his policies, that his support crumbled and the men he had attacked were re-elected with resound-
ing majorities.

15. The most authoritative treatment is found in V. O. Key, Jr., *Politics,
Parties, and Pressure Groups* (4th ed., 1958).

8

THE THEORY AND PRACTICE OF DELEGATED ADMINISTRATION

THE DIVERSITIES OF SOCIAL STRUCTURE, and, more especially, the cultural divisions, have given rise to an issue which has been answered quite differently in different federal systems; it is the issue of who should administer the laws which are made on the federal level. Many Americans assume that *of course* the federal government must do it. For in the United States this has been the established practice. To be sure, in recent years some joint administering has developed, as in agriculture and social security, but even here the federal authorities are largely in control. The rather striking homogeneity of the American people, in spite of regional differences, has made such arrangements seem entirely reasonable, especially as the custom of "senatorial courtesy" as well as the need to cooperate with local party bosses has generally been manifest in the appointments to local federal office. But when the differences are as pronounced as those between the U.S. mainland and Puerto Rico, the demand put forward that federal legislation be administered by the state government is quite natural; yet this idea has aroused much puzzled comment and some sharp criticism. Such comments overlook that at least two of the mature federal countries, Switzerland and Germany, have always operated on the basis of delegating a large part of the administration of federal laws to the canton and *Land* governments, after providing for such delegation in their constitutions.[1]

The issue is a significant one in a number of the newer federal systems, especially those, like India and the European Community, which are being compounded of established governments with more or less highly developed bureaucracies. This was, of course, also the situation of Germany at the time of her unification. The problem presented itself in terms of integrating existing administrative units, as well as utilizing them for the execution of federal legislation. But there was the further problem that Bavarians, for example, did not wish to be "administered" by Prussians, and vice versa; that is to say, Bavarians did not wish to see culturally alien persons, though they were Germans, in their midst. Linguistic aspects—a different dialect—were by no means the only point at issue; many behavioral traits were involved.[2]

To students of federal and regional relations, the questions posed by these experiences pertain, of course, to the advantages and disadvantages in each of these arrangements. Let us review them in turn. Federal execution of all federal policy has the basic advantage of ensuring uniformity throughout the union. If federal officials are responsible for the carrying out of federal policy, it simplifies the problem of control and ensures full accountability; supervision is simply an administrative task. Obviously, then, federal policy cannot easily be frustrated by the local authorities, although where the issue is "hot," and cooperation is required, local officials may find ways of nullifying the efforts of federal officials; it has happened recurrently in the United States, especially in the field of race relations. The advantage of unity and uniformity is bought at the expense of needing very large federal administrative entities. Such extended federal administration has the advantage of providing a strong centralizing force (if that is wanted), but it also has the disadvantages resulting from excessive size. We need not here enter into all the issues that are associated with such "bureaucratization"; suffice it to mention that such federal bureaucracies will cement otherwise disparate units, as happened in Canada, until the French Canadians began to develop a self-consciousness of their own nationality (see above and chapter 15). But there are other disadvantages, especially where the federal system is formed out of pre-existing states, with strong administrative organizations. The problem of transforming local into national services, which took the form of "federalizing" them in both Australia and Canada, is not an easy one. Another major disadvantage is the duplication and overlapping of federal and local administrative services, with consequent waste and inefficiency.[3]

The advantages of effective delegation are, of course, the obverse of the disadvantages just sketched. But perhaps it might be well to indicate very briefly how administrative delegation works in Switzerland and Germany. Not all federal legislation is administered by the cantons and *Länder;* there are functions, especially foreign affairs and defense, which are largely handled on the federal level, though even in these instances there are exceptions, such as cultural relations with foreign countries and the draft of soldiers; there are functions which are delegated in whole or in part. At the same time, "contact" fields, such as taxation and social security (insurance) as well as a great deal of economic policy, are left to the local units. There is detailed provision for this in both constitutions.[4] The constitutions also provide for federal supervision of such administrative activities, and an elaborate code of carefully circumscribed practices has been developed in this connection.

The advantages of such delegated administration are at

least three. First, duplication is avoided. Second, the impact of federal legislation is mediated through locally responsible agencies. Third, it enables the federal authorities to draw on locally entrenched administrative services. This is important primarily when such services already exist. It commits the local authorities to the federal bargain, and enables them to participate effectively in negotiating the federal compromises. Especially when reinforced by an institution such as the German Federal Council (through which the *Länder* cooperate in federal legislation), this may become very effective. For in this Federal Council, though it be formally composed of the Minister Presidents of the several *Länder,* most of the work is actually done by competent officials to whom authority is delegated and who work in special committees with a functional task.[5] Thoroughly familiar with the problems which the execution of federal legislation has caused or will present, they can contribute a good deal to effective integration and coordination. They can also smooth the difficulties which may arise in connection with federal supervision. Nonetheless, it has to be admitted that federal supervision can produce conflict. Indeed, it may (as does federal execution of federal laws in a system such as that of the United States) raise issues of particular bitterness, as has already happened in the European Common Market. Since the local units become in effect the agents of the federal authorities, safeguards are required to make sure that the local officials do not encroach upon the federal sphere; likewise, safeguards are needed to ensure that the federal supervision does not turn into control of the local sphere of competence and jurisdiction. Both are real dangers which only much practical experience can prevent. If the different units execute federal policy in too divergent a way, administrative confusion and even chaos might result; yet, local autonomy may be lost if federal administration seeks to dominate local activities by means of interference, rather than merely to control the faithful execution of federal policy. Effective control requires three instrumentalities. First, there should exist a channel of information by which the federal government can know the manner of the local execution of its policies. Second, the federal authorities ought to have the power to give instructions with reference to the execution of federal policy. And third, the federal government should be provided with some means of compelling obedience to its instructions. In both Switzerland and Germany, these instrumentalities are provided to some extent. On the whole, they have served to make the delegated administration function smoothly, though there are instances of sharp conflict.[6] It can be seen from this review that advantages and disadvantages of both centralized and delegated administration are fairly evenly balanced. Whether one system or the other is preferable depends upon the particular circumstances, especially the degree of cultural and social diversity. "Cooperative federalism" and "sharing" do, in any case, to an increasing extent involve delegated administration in the United States, too. It is also involved to some extent in grant-in-aid patterns of operation, and has become important in social security and medicare administration.

Delegated administration raises, in a sense, the issue of federal decision-making. For as we pointed out above, one of its features is that the officials of the local level are brought into close contact with the officials on the federal level at the initiating stage of federal policy in so far as this is feasible. It is a noteworthy feature of American federalism that this is rarely the case. Sorensen could write his study of presidential decision-making[7] without ever mentioning governors, let alone local officials.

NOTES TO CHAPTER 8

1. See the provisions reprinted in Bowie and Friedrich (eds.), *Studies in Federalism* (1954), chapter 1, pp. 93 ff.

2. See Bowie and Friedrich, *op. cit.*, chapter 2, pp. 78 ff., and the literature there.

3. See chapters 12 and 15 of this volume.

4. See, for example, Article 74, Basic Law of the Federal Republic of Germany.

5. Karl-Heinz Neunreither, *Der Bundestag zwischen Politik und Verwaltung* (1959).

6. Arnold Köttgen, *Der Bundesgesetzgeber und die Gemeinden* (1957). See also his "Der Einfluss des Bundes auf die Deutsche Verwaltung," in *Jahrbuch des Öffentlichen Rechts*, Vol. III (1954), pp 67–147; Dietrich Katzenstein, "Rechtliche Erscheinungsformen der Machtverschiebung zwischen Bund und Ländern seit 1949," in *Die Öffentliche Verwaltung* (1958), pp. 593–604.

7. Theodore C. Sorensen, *The Olive Branch or the Arrow: Decision-Making in the White House* (1963).

9

FEDERAL POLICY AND
DECISION-MAKING

DECISION-MAKING having come to the fore as a focus of political science inquiry,[1] it is surprising that the trends and issues in federal decision-making have received relatively little attention; yet very crucial problems are involved. It is, to be sure, easy to overestimate the importance of deciding upon courses of political action, when actually many political actions are repetitive or adaptive without any decision being involved. Much political behavior is not freely chosen but socially conditioned. Even so, decisions, and more especially policy decisions, are a crucial aspect of federal as of all politics. An authoritarian leader like General de Gaulle objects to supranationality precisely because he resents the prospect of *some* decision being made without or against him. Indeed, the issue of sovereignty is the issue over who has the last word, that is to say, who makes the final decision. A federal order is characterized by the fact that many crucial decisions must be arrived at cooperatively; President Johnson's constant concern with "consensus" is due to his realization of the necessity of such cooperation. He cannot afford to jeopardize the cooperation of those who share in the decision-making power, more especially the Senate's majority. And when Puerto Ricans object to the fact that such important areas as foreign relations and defense are being decided upon without their effective cooperation, they are rightly questioning the present status of the federal relationship. For it is the essence of such a relationship that the component units share as such in the determination of federal policy. They do so in the United States in a somewhat attenuated way through their equal representation in the Senate. How then are political decisions in a federal system arrived at? Before we can adumbrate an answer to that question, it is necessary to elaborate what kind of political decisions there are.

Broadly speaking, three types of political decisions may be distinguished. First, there is the decision of a single individual deciding a matter wholly within his range of power and authority. This kind of decision-making may be further subdivided into those made with and those made without advice. Such decisions are typically those of the administrator and of the citizen. The second kind is arrived at by a group's joint action, either unanimously or by majority, after extended consultation among its members. Courts, commissions, legislative committees, and numerous other bodies acting without public participation employ this kind of procedure. The third type is one made in the light of public discussion and argument. Town meetings and party conclaves, legislating and budget-making fall into this category. One might designate these three types as individual, group, and public decisions. Differentiated by procedure and scope of application, they have in common that they are decisions about what action to take in face of a problem confronting the decision-maker or those for whom he is acting.[2]

The taking of action can be seen as a process which may be broken down into a number of stages. Lasswell has distinguished seven such stages or functions: They are as much

the stages of a policy-making as of a decision-making process;
indeed, the two tend to merge into each other. For policy is a
deliberately adopted decision as to how to act in an ongoing
situation.[3] There is the intelligence phase of gathering information, of trying to predict and to plan; there is the
recommendation phase, which involves the promotion of
alternatives; there is the prescription phase, which results in
the prescribing of general rules; this is followed by the invoca-
tion phase, in the course of which conduct is invoked in
accordance with the rules; there is the application phase, in
which conduct is definitively specified as according to the
rules; finally there are the assessment and termination phases,
during which success and failure of the policy and its possible
termination are decided upon. It is apparent that only the
first three phases are, strictly speaking, relevant to one kind
of decision-making, the making of rules, whereas the later
phases constitute other kinds. For the making of rules and the
adoption of policies is only one kind of decision, and the
procedures indicated above suggest that different kinds of
processes may be suitable to different kinds of decisions. Addi-
tionally, the study of decision-making may seek to elucidate
the "setting"—an inquiry which leads once more into the
kind of problems which have been explored earlier (chapters 7
and 8); value orientations, institutional pattern, role differentiation and related aspects would here become relevant.[4]

If one projects this general pattern of decision-making
against the background of a federal order, it appears that the
processes and functions are both more complicated and more
refined. Individual decisions are multiplied, not only because
the citizen has to decide twice on many issues, but also because there is a multiplication of "chief executives." Group
decisions of a particular kind are needed, because in numerous policy contexts it becomes necessary to organize specific
decision-making groups representing regions or other subdivisions. Finally, public decisions usually involve extensive
exploration by bodies on the two levels. In all these spheres,

a federal policy will have to evolve a large number of specific rules of procedure, behavioral habits, and the like. The descriptive literature on federal countries is replete with illustrations. We have already mentioned "senatorial courtesy" in the United States; Switzerland has developed firm traditions about the proportions in which the three linguistic groups must be represented in all governmental activities; Germany has elaborated its Federal Council with its complex ritual of interstate cooperation for providing federal policy decisions with adequate regional support.

On the whole, though, the sharp separation of federal and state functions has tended to minimize the participation of the component units in the federal sphere of decision-making. Only constitutional amendments are formally identified as decisions requiring such collaboration. Cooperative federalism has increased the collaborative scope, but it is quite typical that as important a decision as that in the U.S. Steel case of 1962 was arrived at without significant sharing by governors or other state authorities.[5] The situation is, of course, different in cases of policy involving "states' rights" and, more especially, the problems of segregation in the United States. In such cases, efforts at coordinating federal decisions with state decision-making may be crucial for the success of a particular policy.

As pointed out in the discussion of delegated administration, a federal system built on administrative delegation is more apt to institutionalize effective interaction between the two levels of government. Both the flow of information and the recommendation of policy alternatives will contain a significant amount of local participation. This fact may have both positive and negative results; for it is bound to slow up (and may possibly prevent) the making of decisions, as has certainly been the case in the Federal Republic; it may also lead to the adoption of decisions which more nearly meet the needs of the situation.

The High Commission of the Common Market has gathered some extremely interesting experience on the subject of federal decision-making in a very loose federal setup. Until General de Gaulle decided not to cooperate any longer (that is, made the basic decision to abandon important parts of the federal bargain), the decisions of the High Commission, requiring the approval of the Ministerial Council acting by unanimity, necessitated a very extended consultation, which included the securing of competent advice, for the purpose of "defining the situation." This defining of the situation by perception, choice, and expectation[6] is done primarily in terms of the federal relationship itself; it cannot be accomplished without full exploration of the values, interests, and beliefs of the federated entities involved in the issue at hand. A special difficulty in such federal decision-making results from the fact that the several federated units are interacting and that what appears as a given at the outset of a policy discussion may undergo radical change as the positions of other entities become clear. Thus General de Gaulle's threat of noncooperation, in December, 1964, if his specific timetable and policy preferences were not met (leaving aside the legal and institutional conditions and qualifications), produced a change of German orientation which permitted a compromise on the uniform grain prices, in spite of the contrary interests of German grain producers. In more fully integrated federal systems this aspect of federal decision-making leads to the formation of blocs for specific policy purposes in the decision-making bodies and groups. By such moves it is intended to forestall the possible breaking away of some entities where complex interest patterns are involved.

It remains to say a word about the extent to which experience with decision-making promotes the evolution of institutions. It is unfortunately the fashion to juxtapose behavioral and institutional studies as if they were radically separate and apart. But just as institutions provide part of the setting or environment of decisions, so decisions tend to mold and reshape institutions. For institutions are basically nothing but habitual behavior patterns which may be reinforced by rules. In federal orders, policies which require local implementation will typically result from decisions which reinforce the centripetal tendencies, while the opposite is true of policies which do not, for example, foreign and defense policy decisions. Such decisions and policies unify, while social and cultural policies diversify.

NOTES TO CHAPTER 9

1. See my *Man and His Government* (1963), chapter 3, and the studies cited there, especially those by Lasswell, Snyder, and Furniss. There now exist extensive bibliographies on the subject; Karl W. Deutsch, *The Nerves of Government—Models of Political Communication and Control*, Part III (1963), has reviewed this literature, especially in chapter 9.

2. Friedrich, *op. cit.* (note 1 above), pp. 79 ff.

3. See Daniel Lerner and Harold D. Lasswell (eds.), *The Policy Sciences: Recent Developments in Scope and Method* (1951). Lasswell later put forward his view in *The Decision Process*, Government Research Bureau, University of Maryland (1956).

4. See Richard C. Snyder, H. W. Bruck, and Burtin Sapin, *Decision-Making as an Approach to the Study of International Politics*, Foreign Policy Analysis Project of Princeton University (1954); on p. 34 the authors present a diagram of this process.

5. See Grant McConnell, *Steel and the Presidency, 1962* (1963), which does not mention the federal aspect at all; a foreign reader might believe that the United States is a unitary state.

6. Snyder *et al.*, *op. cit.* (note 4 above), pp. 37 f. and 47 f.

10

INTERNATIONAL FEDERALISM?

THERE ARE THOSE who would deny that there is any such thing as international federalism, urging a sharp differentiation between the federalism of a federal state and the internationalism of a confederation of states. Indeed this distinction used to be the quintessence of the static and formalistic approach. It still survives in much popular discussion and propaganda. The struggle over supranationalism in the European Economic Community (the Common Market) shows that the dichotomy has political meaning and significance. There can be little question that a distinction needs to be made between a federal order which represents a unit toward the outside and faces other states as if it were a unitary system and a federal order which does not. There are, however, times when it may be very difficult to say whether one or the other situation prevails. Thus the several Soviet Republics represented in the United Nations face other states as distinct entities, yet they are part of a closely-knit federal system. Comparably complex, though in the opposite sense, is the situation of the British Commonwealth, which sometimes does, and at other times does not, represent itself as a unit toward other states.

It is therefore desirable both to recognize the existence of international federalism and not to misunderstand it as a sharply defined alternative to national federalism. Federal orders range, as was pointed out many years ago, over a wide spectrum between the nonfederal limits of a unitary state and a plurality of states. They are all part of the general process that federalism is and involves.[1]

The qualifying of a federal order as "international" is here taken to mean that a particular federal order is sufficiently loose for its members to have separate and autonomous relations with other states and, at the same time, to develop or maintain joint relations. The European nations united in the European communities (the European Economic Community, Euratom, and the European Coal and Steel Community) are facing the outside both together and separately; that is why the EEC is an instance of international federalism. Another instance, moving in the opposite direction, is the British Commonwealth.[2] In connection with the federal relations of Puerto Rico, the distinction is a hotly debated one; those who advocate a separate and autonomous relation of Puerto Rico with other states, whether throughout the world or in a more limited area, are to that extent raising the issue of international federalism. It does not mean an end to the federal relationship, but it does mean a highly significant qualitative alteration in the nature of the relationship.[3]

International federalism has played an important role in the building of national states as well as in organizing an international order. It has also served to facilitate the transition from empire and imperialism to cooperation and equality. The most interesting example of a gradual substitution of a federation for an empire is, of course, the transformation of the British Empire into the British Commonwealth of Nations.[4] This feat was accomplished very gradually as former colonies were granted the status of dominions, beginning with Canada in 1867. A dominion today is a nearly independent state, of course, tied to Great Britain by bonds of common political and legal tradition as symbolized in the crown, for even India accepts the crown as a symbol, though, as a republic, it does not accept allegiance to the crown. Many would deny the federal character of the Commonwealth; if one does not accept the reality of international federalism, this is indeed a cogent argument.[5] But then the EEC would certainly also have to be ruled out as a federal order, since in many respects the bonds of the Community of the Six are less secure than are those of the Commonwealth. By skillful bargaining and pragmatic compromise—the proverbial muddling through—the British have succeeded in holding the Commonwealth together. They have provided the essentials of federal equality of the component "mechanism" of this federal (or confederal, if preferred) order in the Commonwealth Prime Ministers' Conference, which has operated reasonably effectively as an instrumentality for discussing and, when possible, adopting common action. The gradual evolution of this federal relationship or bond within the Commonwealth, with all its subtle gradations even between present members, suggests a lesson for all those who would structure such a relationship "irrevocably" or "unalterably."

For all governments and hence all federal orders, the establishment and maintenance of an effective executive is decisive; it presents particular difficulties in international federal schemes. And yet, there can be little doubt that the success or failure of the federalizing process depends upon this factor more than any other. Historical evidence in support of this general proposition is abundant. This is not to say that the organizing of such an effective executive guarantees the success of federal order; obstacles and, more especially, divisive forces, may be too strong for real progress. Even then such an executive may be able to ensure the effective execution of the existing federal bargain. The history of the United Nations provides a case in point;[6] the EEC may find itself forced to be content with a similar operation for a certain period. In any case, the setting up of an executive is crucial for an international federal order, and for the retention of such an order in the event the federalizing process operates toward greater independence rather than closer union. In such situations, the advantage of a developed and responsible bureaucracy may be decisive, regardless of how the chief executive is chosen.

Closed federal systems usually exclude secession, but many federal systems have had to face the problem of the admission of new members. In international federal setups, secession is typically provided for; it may be merely a formal right, as is the right of secession of the member states in the Soviet Union.[7] It stands to reason that the looser a federal order is, the more readily will it admit new members *and* allow old members to secede. As the case of the United States shows, there may be special reasons for readily admitting new members into a close-knit federal union but, in such a union, secession will be excluded. The War between the States, as well as the *Sonderbund* War in Switzerland (1847), was waged to prevent secession of members that wished to secede because they felt that they could not accept a key policy decision of the majority. Leaving legal provisions aside, it can be stated generally that the ability to secede will increase with the weakness of the federal bond. One might be tempted to make it the distinguishing criteria of an international federal union. But such a distinction does not always hold, though it is undoubtedly often true. The ability to secede will decline and tend to disappear as the inclusive community is extended to ever-widening spheres of governmental activity. The EEC presents an interesting, if somewhat irregular case here. Since the Treaty of Rome (1957) no admission has occurred, though association has been negotiated; secession is not permitted by the Treaty; yet France, under De Gaulle (though blocking the admission of Britain), has hinted at her own secession. Puerto Rico's situation is in a sense illuminated by these observations: While her admission to the federal union of the United States is, if a possibility at all, only a distant prospect, her secession has been viewed as entirely possible by President and Congress alike. Whether a more permanent federal relationship should retain the right to secession would seem to be bound up with the question of how close the relationship itself is; that at least would be in keeping with the general practice of federalism.

International federalism also raises complex issues in connection with a common citizenship. Obviously, federal states will have such common citizenship; there is an interesting and symptomatic contrast, though, in that some federal states provide for a person being a citizen of the union as a consequence of his being a citizen of one of the member states, while others make citizenship in a member unit depend upon federal citizenship. Obviously the latter is a feature of a closer union, as the case of Germany shows; there, originally the former arrangement was used; today, the latter prevails, as it also does in the United States. In the reverse process of increasing federal differentiation, as in the British Commonwealth, common citizenship may disappear altogether; hence local citizenship as a condition of federal citizenship may become suitable at a certain point in the evolution.

The question has been raised, in regard to Puerto Rico, whether common citizenship imposes certain limits on a federal relationship. The usual answer has been that such citizenship presupposes that the union be a unit in international relations, and it has been deduced from that that at least foreign relations and defense must be federally controlled if common citizenship is to be justified. While this may well be the practical consequence of American and more specifically congressional attitudes, it is hard to see how it follows from the federal relationship as such. There may be fairly close bonds without common citizenship, as in the EEC; there may be very loose ones with such common citizenship, as was the case at one point in the evolution of the Commonwealth.[8] The drafters of the constitution for the proposed European Political Community left the question of formal citizenship open, while its rights were gradually to be extended to more and more persons.[9] This was included despite the fact that the draft constitution provided for only the "coordination" of the foreign policies of the member states.[10] Such a provision shows that there is no intrinsic reason why common citizenship should imply a united foreign policy. In short, citizenship, while an important feature of federal orders, is not a presupposition of such a relationship, nor can the "limits" of such a relationship be derived from common citizenship. It all depends upon the circumstances. But it is possible to formulate a rule of thumb to the effect that the more international a federal relationship becomes, the more questionable becomes the retention of common citizenship.

By way of a conclusion, I would add that it has been argued recently that, in the EEC, "beyond the express treaty requirements for the observance of federal fidelity, the federal nature of the structure requires federal fidelity and federal-mindedness in other cases as well."[11] The issues of federal fidelity, comity, spirit, and behavior will be discussed somewhat more at length below (chapter 23); here it suffices to record agreement with the above author's consequent conclusion that "the supranational power is not subject to limitations of national constitutional law, including those which guarantee the position of the states."[12] But what if one of the partners refuses to assent? The question highlights the fact that in such arrangements as those constituting the European Communities there remains an element of *international* authority.[13] Hence the term "international federalism" would seem to be justified for designating such novel arrangements. (See chapter 21.)

NOTES TO CHAPTER 10

1. See *Systems of Integrating the International Community,* ed. Elmer Plischke (1964), especially the chapter by Francis O. Wilcox, "International Confederation—the United Nations and State Sovereignty," pp. 27–66, and my own paper on international federalism.

2. Patrick Gordon-Walker, *The Commonwealth* (1962); for an interesting contrasting continental European evaluation, see G. Treves, *Il Commonwealth britannico* (1949).

3. Carl J. Friedrich, *Puerto Rico—Middle Road to Freedom* (1959), chapter 3. This possibility is completely overlooked by Gordon Lewis, *Puerto Rico* (1963). See also a comprehensive and balanced study, Henry Wells, *Modernization and Leadership in Puerto Rico* (1968), especially chapters 11 and 12.

4. *Federalism in the Commonwealth,* ed. William S. Livingston (1963) does not include this aspect, but it is treated by Taylor Cole in the paper "Federalism in the Commonwealth," *Public Policy,* Vol. XIV (1965), pp. 355–79.

5. K. C. Wheare, *The Constitutional Structure of the Commonwealth* (1960); Patrick Gordon-Walker, *op. cit.;* D. B. Miller, *The Commonwealth and the World* (1958).

6. Wilcox, *op. cit.* (note 1 above), pp. 40–45. See also Inis L. Claude, *Swords into Plowshares* (rev. ed. 1959), chapter 10.

7. Carl J. Friedrich, "Admission of New States, Territorial Adjustments and Secession," Study 15 in Bowie and Friedrich, *op. cit.* (note 1, chapter 1), pp. 752–89.

8. Clive Parry, *Naturalization and Citizenship Laws of the Commonwealth and the Republic of Ireland* (1957), chapters 2 and 3.

9. The Draft Resolutions of the Study Committee (1952) had proposed that "all the citizens of the member states shall be citizens of the Community." See Bowie and Friedrich, *op. cit.* (note 1, chapter 1), p. 819; see also in the same work Study 12, a comparative study on citizenship by W. J. Schrenk.

10. Article 69.

11. Peter Hay, *Federalism and Supranational Organizations: Patterns for New Legal Structures* (1966), p. 202.

12. Hay, *op. cit.,* p. 295.

13. Dusan Sidjanski, in an interesting volume some years ago, suggested that this kind of federalism be called "amphyctionique." *Fédéralisme Amphyctionique—Éléments de système et tendance internationale* (1956).

11

THE ISSUE OF
FEDERAL ASSOCIATION

INTERNATIONAL FEDERALISM provides the background for the many-faceted potentialities of associated membership with a federal union, however close. Although association has been known to have occurred in the past, notably in connection with the leagues of city states, it has come into its own only in the twentieth century and in conjunction with the full development of federalism. Its quintessence is the institutionalized process by which a state becomes associated with an existing federal union by means of organizing a looser federal relationship than that prevailing among the regular members of the union.[1] Its direct ancestor is the institution of the *"Zugewandte" Orte* (associated places) in the ancient Swiss Confederation. Its outstanding examples at present are Puerto Rico, the associates of the Common Market—Greece, Turkey and some African states (federated for this purpose)—and the Free City of Berlin, associated with the Federal Republic of Germany. The reasons for arranging such looser association may be many: greater cultural difference, interference of a foreign power, desire for greater neutrality, and so forth. Generally and abstractly stated, the case for associated as against full membership can be put thus: When the weight and number of common values and interests is less, and/or the weight and number of divergent values and interests is more than is the case for regular members, associated membership is indicated.

In spite of the historical antecedents, it is fair to say that free association is a new dimension of federalism, suggesting that there even could be an inner and outer group of participating communities, such as seems to be developing in the process of European unification. The idea that an autonomous, self-governing community might be an "associated" member of a federal union is difficult to understand and to interpret as long as federalism is seen merely as a static pattern or design, rather than being comprehended also as an ongoing process. If the federal order is understood as continually evolving, then the involvement of an associated member becomes part of this over-all development. Neither permanence nor irrevocability are part of the federal relationship, according to the more recent insight into the nature of federalism (see chapters 1 and 23). Once this is understood, it also becomes patent that the peculiar relationship of association requires effective institutionalization just as much as does full membership. The typical functions of developed government, the executive, legislative, and judicial spheres of action, must all be provided for. What is perhaps less evident, there must also be available, as under all constitutionalism, and more particularly under its federal form, a sound system of organized change; the great discovery of the need for an amending power which the drafters of the American Constitution made[2] has particular application to the federal relationship of association. At the same time, the insight of the men of Philadelphia that such an amending power must itself express the federal relationship, and therefore must constitutionally fix the participation of the members, applies equally to the case of associated membership.

This need is particularly clearly recognized in the treaties of association concluded between outside powers and the European Economic Community (Common Market).[3] Requests have also been filed for such association by Austria, Denmark, Ireland, Israel, Norway, Spain, Sweden, and Switzerland, as well as some other new states.[4] Some of these would prefer membership, notably Denmark, Norway, and Ireland, whereas Austria, Sweden, and Switzerland, because of their policy of neutrality, definitely desire association rather than membership; the same, for other reasons, holds for the African states. In the case of these as well as of Greece and Turkey, it has been urged that even though the existing relations of Greece and Turkey with the members of EEC might suggest membership, "their economic structures are so different from those of the Six, that a gradual process of association leading in a more or less distant future to full membership seemed a better solution."[5] The agreements which were finally concluded (in accordance with articles 237 and 238 of the EEC Treaty) regulating association of Greece and Turkey, in 1961 and 1963, respectively, were the result of long and careful negotiations which established "a framework of relations, based on the progressive creation of a customs union and an economic union of exactly the same kind as that prescribed for implementing the Treaty within the Community."[6] These agreements contain many detailed provisions of an economic sort, but what is of immediate interest is that there is set up, in each case, a Council of the Association which is charged with administering and developing the association. Meeting at least once every six months, it is assisted by an executive committee which acts on the basis of equality (Greece has as many members as has the Community) and it has already accomplished important work in implementing the agreements.[7] Besides the Council and its executive committee, a Parliamentary Commission has been established to provide the opportunity for continuing consultation of the parliamentary control bodies as the necessary liaison with the national parliaments.

A very similar institutional framework has been brought into being for the association of African states (Burundi, Cameroun, Central African Republic, the two Congo Republics, Ivory Coast, Dahomey, Gabon, Upper Volta, Malagasy Republic, Mali, Mauritania, Niger, Rwanda, Senegal, Chad, and Togo) federated for this purpose as the "associated states."[8] It too consists of a Council of Association (with committee), a Parliamentary Conference, and a Court of Arbitration. The Council in this case consists of a representative of each of the member states of the Community and of each of the associated states, as well as members of the Commission of EEC; it can act only with a majority of all members present. Meeting once a year, the Council of Association is assisted by a committee, also based on equal representation, which meets more often, prepares its decisions, and works in accordance with the Council's regulations; it can act for the Council, when so authorized. Provided with a regular secretariat, these bodies have already done important work in implementing and interpreting the association agreement. The Parliamentary Conference receives an annual report from the Council and can make recommendations in the form of resolutions. The Court of Arbitration is called upon only after the Council has failed to reach a settlement. It consists of five members, two nominated by the Council of the EEC, two by the associated states, and a president named by the Council of Association. Court members are expected to be independent and competent and to serve during the life of the agreement. The Court's decisions are by majority and are binding upon the parties.

It may seem a bit farfetched to speak of India, Pakistan,

and Malaysia as associated members of the Commonwealth—
in law they are considered members—and yet that seems to be
their position in fact; for the federal bond linking them to
the other members of the Commonwealth is reduced to
acceptance of the Crown as "the symbol of the free association of its independent member nations"; "common allegiance
to the Crown" is held to be incompatible with their republican form of government,[9] but they accept the Queen as "Head
of the Commonwealth." In their case, the relationship is
almost completely informal. No institutional arrangements
are spelled out, although their prime ministers do participate
in the Prime Ministers' Conference. The case is mentioned
here primarily in order to indicate how very tenuous, indeed,
the federal relationship under association can become, when
political, economic, and cultural developments weaken it. It
is also well to bear in mind the great skill which British states-
manship has brought to the task of maintaining a relationship
under highly adverse conditions. The Puerto Rican case
seems hardly to fit this pattern at the present time, but conditions may change, and the maintenance of an association may
yet be preferable to complete separation and independence.

The case of Berlin within the Federal Republic is different,
but nonetheless instructive. Here we have an entity which
would very much prefer to form an integral part of the larger
federal union that is the Federal Republic, but is prevented
from doing so by Allied veto and the East-West conflict. As a
consequence, West Berlin is tied to the Federal Republic in a
free association (not called thus) which gives her citizens the
citizenship of the Federal Republic and full opportunity to
participate in its political life provides for the location of
important federal German administrative and judicial bodies
in Berlin, and permits Berlin to send to the federal legislative
bodies representatives who fully take part in the work, although they do not have a formal vote. (There is an exception
to this voting arrangement in that Berlin delegates can vote

in the presidential elections, which are carried out through a special assembly.)[10] All federal laws are applicable to Berlin, although upon Allied insistence they have to be re-enacted by the Berlin legislature. Of course Berlin, like all other states of the Federal Republic, administers (executes) many federal laws and is in this connection subject to federal supervision. Judicial decisions are integrated into Federal Republic precedents, and cases are appealed to the highest Federal Republic courts, such as the Constitutional Court, one of which the Federal Administrative Court or *Bundesverwaltungsgericht,* is located in Berlin. Berlin is obviously a case where the citizens have a maximal desire to share in the federal union; their position corresponds to that of the inhabitants of an incorporated American territory prior to its achieving statehood. But unlike those territories, Berlin was in the past an integral part of Germany, indeed its capital, and the only reason for its being prevented from rejoining the federal union is the division of the country, supported by force of arms of the Soviet Union.[11] Its federal association with the Federal Republic is consequently international in the most literal sense.

It is probably more in keeping with the basically different position of the political systems involved to derive the more general lesson of a need for effective instrumentalities of steady cooperation and continuing change. A formal institutionalized bond calls for the possibility of amending it by mutual agreement between the partners. All legislation should be based upon cooperative arrangements; Berlin's scheme of re-enacting the federal laws before they become applicable makes sense under such circumstances; in the EEC this is the common practice of the member countries as well as of associates. It might, however, be sufficient to provide the associated member with the power to declare any federal law inapplicable. Furthermore, an associated member of a federal union should be provided with the maximum amount of delegated administration (see chapter 5); here again the experience in the loose union that is the EEC suggests the broadest application. Perhaps the most difficult question which remains is that of the associated state's tie-in with the federal union's foreign relations and defense policies. In the case of Berlin, until recently practically complete acceptance of the Federal Republic's decisions was a natural consequence not only of Berlin's dependence upon West Germany, but also of her citizens' firm desire to remain a part of the German people and its political order. In the case of the EEC, foreign policy and defense have so far not been effectively federalized,[12] but even this possibility has caused Austria a major headache in connection with her association; for the "neutrality" which the State Treaty of 1955 provides excludes Austria from entering into common defense or foreign policies; the same would presumably apply to Switzerland, if she sought association with the EEC, as quite a few Swiss demand. The very hesitancy of the EEC to enter this field facilitates association. In the case of Puerto Rico, the close-knit federalism of the United States makes it a serious problem. And yet, some kind of equivalent for the current participation of the citizens of American states in the shaping of foreign and defense policies would seem to be indicated.[13] Treaties might be made subject to specific assent, legislative control participated in, and some body corresponding to the Commonwealth Prime Ministers' Conference might be established.

NOTES TO CHAPTER 11

1. Association, a novel feature of contemporary federalism as it is being elaborated even for close-knit federal states, has not to my knowledge received to date the careful comparative analysis it deserves, but such a study has now been initiated. See the comments in my two papers: "New Tendencies in Federal Theory and Practice," in *Jahrbuch des Öffentlichen Rechts*, New Series, Vol. 14 (1965), pp. 1 ff; and "International Federalism in Theory and Practice," in *Systems of Integrating the International Community*, ed. Elmer Plischke (1964), pp. 117 ff., especially pp. 152 ff. The French Constitution of 1958 contained an article (Article 88) on association which has not been

applied; it may have been hoped that it would help solve the Algerian problem.

2. It is not sufficiently appreciated how novel this provision really was. See my *Constitutional Government and Democracy* (4th ed., 1968), chapter VIII.

3. See European Economic Commission, *Sixth General Report* (1962–63), pp. 190 ff.; and *Seventh General Report* (1963–64), pp. 222 ff. and 259 ff. See also *European Yearbook,* Vol. IX (1961), pp. 453–503, giving the text of the Treaty of Association with Greece; *ibid.,* Vol. X(2) (1962), p. 793; and *ibid.* Vol. XI(2) (1963), pp. 511 ff. and 607 ff.

4. *Sixth General Report,* pp. 236 ff.; *Seventh General Report,* pp. 266 ff.

5. *European Yearbook,* Vol. XI (1963), pp. 58–59.

6. *Ibid.,* p. 59.

7. *Seventh General Report,* pp. 259 ff.

8. The Treaty of Association is given in *European Yearbook,* Vol. XI(2) (1963), pp. 622 ff. The articles on the institutions (Articles 39–53) are on pp. 632 ff.

9. See Wheare, *op. cit.* (note 10, chapter 1), chapter VII.

10. Article 54 of the Basic Law.

11. See W. Phillips Davison, *The Berlin Blockade—A Study in Cold War Politics* (1958), especially chapter XI; Hans Speier, *Divided Berlin: The Anatomy of Soviet Political Blackmail* (1961); Peter H. Merkl, *The Origin of the West German Republic* (1963), especially pp. 63 ff.

12. Karl-Heinz Neunreither, *Das Europa der Sechs ohne Aussenpolitik* (1964).

13. For more detailed argument, see the discussion in my *Puerto Rico,* pp. 68 ff. For background, see Charles T. Goodsell, *Administration of a Revolution—Executive Reform in Puerto Rico under Governor Tugwell, 1941–1946* (1965).

PART II

Case Studies

12

AUSTRALIA:
FEDERAL PARLIAMENTARIANISM

THE FOLLOWING CASE STUDIES, each focused on a particular country, are not meant to be either exhaustive or definitive; they are intended to highlight an issue, rather than to give a complete panorama of the particular federal regime. Such completeness would be impossible within the limited space of a single volume and there already exist descriptive monographs, which the notes indicate. Here the emphasis is upon the analysis of an outstanding feature which provides empirical evidence for a basic problem's handling in a specific context. Their alphabetical arrangement is purely a matter of convenience.

Australia is of particular interest because its federal regime is at the same time a functioning parliamentary system. This is a challenge, because it has for some time been argued that it is hard to combine a federal regime with a parliamentary executive of the British cabinet type. It is so combined in Canada, Australia, and the Federal Republic of Germany. But considerable difficulties result from the fact that the relation between the opposition and the government is thereby given an almost uninterrupted chance of erupting into an electoral struggle. For, under conditions of traditional parliamentary dependency of the cabinet, elections may be called on the national as well as on the local level at any time, and the resulting multiplication, and unpredictable timetable, of elections becomes all the more unmanageable as the number of component units increases.

There is a further complication on the national level which points in the same direction. A federal regime presupposes bicameral representation, since the component units are and must be represented in a separate body, be it senate or council. The cabinet can then be made dependent upon the confidence of either one house or the other, or both. If one house is chosen, it is necessarily given a predominant position which is apt to endanger the federal balance; if both are chosen, instability results. As a consequence, it would seem that a federal regime ought, from a practical viewpoint, avoid the classic parliamentary system. The commitment of both European and British Commonwealth countries to this system is so firm, however, that it has been adopted time and again. When the consequences of such a choice have become apparent, the discussion of possible reforms has rarely, if ever, concerned itself with the desirability of substituting a stable (presidential) for a parliamentary executive. The strength of the parliamentary tradition has been so great that what has been demanded is the abolition of federalism. This has been typically the case in Australia,[1] although recent centrifugal tendencies point in the opposite direction.

Australia's federal union is composed of six states—New South Wales, Victoria, Queensland, South Australia, Western Australia, and Tasmania—and two territories—the Northern Territory and the Australian Capital Territory. Its constitution is a blend of British, American, and Swiss elements, with the latter two of course predominant in the federal features. "We have the American constitution, the Swiss constitution, and slabs of the Canadian constitution hurled at us from all sides *ad nauseam*," exclaimed one of the delegates to the constitutional convention in exasperation. That was true enough, but it resulted in what seems yet, in spite of continuous dissatisfaction in Australia, to be the most nearly balanced combination of federalism and parliamentarianism.

The office of Governor General is largely ceremonial. The chief executive is the Prime Minister, who is dependent upon a parliamentary majority in a lower house that is based upon popular elections. The result has been, inevitably, that this house has become predominant. The upper house, or Senate, is composed of an equal number of senators from each state, and it used to go along with the lower house. The reason was, of course, the party base of the Government. Hence the original expectation that the Senate would protect the states' interests has been slow in materializing. Recently, the Senate has asserted its position more vigorously. This has complicated the situation for the Government. Thoughtful students of these developments feel[2] that it is now virtually impossible for the Government to maintain a majority in the Senate. The balance in this chamber since the election of 1967 is held by the Democratic Labor Party, which campaigned in favor of states' rights. Several senators have developed such strong local support that they are able to defy party discipline.

Even though the national government has suffered significant defeats in the Senate and in efforts to have the constitution amended, its power has grown in the course of the years, though not nearly fast enough to satisfy the advocates of changing to a unitary state: many amendments pointing in this direction have been defeated over the years. These defeats have typically occurred at the local level, since amendments have to be approved by popular referendum.[3] Many of the votes have been close, and the extension of power has been accomplished by less formal means than amendment of the constitution: through judicial interpretation, implementing legislation, and political conventions. But the fact remains that majority sentiment in Australia continues to support the federal scheme of things; indeed, this sentiment has become stronger. The public is willing to pay the price.

A major attack upon the federal scheme was launched by one writer, who argued that federalism and "responsible government" were incompatible. The term responsible government is, of course, imprecise and misleading; Switzerland and the United States also have a truly responsible government; only the pattern of responsibility is different, that is, the executive cannot be "overthrown" by the representative assembly.[4] But this is a rather crude device, and there exist many other ways of enforcing responsibility. Nonetheless, the argument has been cast in terms such as these: that under federalism, the responsibility of the government is impaired. This result, the author believed, was due to the fact that where power is divided, responsibility is divided; because no one can say for sure who is to blame, it is hard to bring anyone to account for what goes wrong. We are told that "no one to this day, has realistically examined this provocative argument."[5] But does this argument really need to be challenged on empirical grounds? If it were a true argument, there never would have been responsible government; for in all constitutional systems, no matter how constructed, power is divided, though in varying degrees and ways.

In a system of responsible parliamentary government, the prime minister and his cabinet will be able to direct the policy decisions of the parliamentary body to whom they are responsible, precisely because that body controls the existence of those who lead and direct them. The leaders of such a national government are therefore necessarily the leaders of the party or coalition which commands a majority. They naturally find irksome the limitations which a constitution—by definition a system of effective regularized restraints[6]—imposes upon their action. Hence it is not surprising that cabinet after

cabinet in Australia has sought to alter the constitution to re-
move some of these limitations. "They seek to make their administration more effective," it has been cogently written,
"and to put through the policies they advocate by the only
means open to them—that of altering the distribution of
powers which they conceive to be an obstacle to their success."[7] It is quite natural that governments should try this; it
is equally significant that as long as the federal spirit is alive
such moves are likely to be defeated.

One interesting federal feature of the Australian cabinet
system is its regard for the territorial distribution of posts. It
is now generally accepted as a convention that all the states
should be, and on a roughly proportional basis, represented
in the national cabinet. This concern is facilitated by the
small number of states. It would be manifestly impossible for
the same convention to prevail in the United States or Switzerland; rather, regions or cultural groupings are similarly
respected there. Such representation is no doubt based upon
the federally organized party system, which requires the satisfaction of local power centers. But this factor should not be
overestimated. As Louise Overacker has written: "In spite of
its federal structure and a strong sense of particularism . . .
unified, disciplined parties with Commonwealth-wide organizations developed."[8] Hence it is not surprising that the cabinet is composed of the leading members of the majority party
in the House of Representatives. They are formally chosen by
the Prime Minister, but are in fact selected in caucus, at least
in the Labor Party, with some discretion remaining with the
Prime Minister in distributing the departments among them.
Even so, the Prime Minister's position has become dominant,
although not as much so as in Britain, and the ancient saying
about his being *primus inter pares* has become rather doubtful. The long-time Prime Minister Sir Robert Menzies came
to dominate the party conclaves as well as the cabinet. His
successor was not able to do so to the same extent.

The cabinet alone can propose expenditures to be made by the treasury, and has a virtual monopoly over the initiation of legislation. Since the cabinet consists of the leaders of the majority party, this is natural enough. Moreover it is in keeping with the trend everywhere, including systems with stable executives, such as the Swiss and the American. There are, of course, also technical reasons for this development.

The cabinet's role in financial matters highlights a feature of Australian federalism[9] which has been the source of continued bitter controversy: the fiscal predominance of the national over the state governments. This predominance expresses itself in very large grants from the national government to the states (nearly A$ 1 billion in 1966). It constitutes a development certainly not foreseen by the men who made the Australian constitution, although the provision for it (Article 96) is broad and explicit. It is clear that such a provision serves to buttress national government leadership as effectuated through the party system. In the earlier part of this century, the national government, through action of parliament, took over the debts of the states a few times. Since 1927, a Loan Council has worked out the national loan policy; the Commonwealth is in a strong, but by no means dominant position in this council, on which the state governments as well as the Commonwealth are represented. All told, the federal system appears to continue quite vigorously, and the recent centrifugal trend fits the oscillation characteristic of a dynamic federalism.

The student of the federalizing process need not be disturbed by the significant long-time evolution toward greater power of the central government that has occurred in Australia during the near seven decades of her constitutional development.[10] He notes that federalism and parliamentarianism have not managed for many years to coexist and to give Australia a rather stable federal government, the component units of which are, like the national government, based upon cabinet responsibility to elected representatives. It is a significant achievement of more than local significance.

NOTES TO CHAPTER 12

1. There does not exist a detailed examination of this problem, but the fairly rich literature on Australian government, politics, and federalism contains much of the basic material and argument. S. Encel, *Cabinet Government in Australia* (1962); L. F. Crisp, *Australian National Government* (1966); and J. D. B. Miller, *Australian Government and Politics* (1954), are good. See also the select bibliography in Bowie and Friedrich, *op. cit.* (note 1, chapter 1), p. 858; and the fine bibliographical essay, S. R. Davis and C. A. Hughes, "Federalism in Australia," in *Federalism in the Commonwealth,* ed. William S. Livingston (1963), pp. 29–57, especially pp. 38 ff.

2. Professor John Powers' helpful suggestions deserve grateful acknowledgment at this point.

3. William S. Livingston, *Federalism and Constitutional Change* (1956), chapter 3, especially pp. 128 ff.

4. The challenge was made by A. P. Canaway, *The Failure of Federalism in Australia* (1930). See also A. H. Birch, *Representative and Responsible Government—An Essay on the British Constitution* (1964), especially chapters 10–13 and 17. On the general problems, see my article "Public Policy and the Nature of Administrative Responsibility," in *Public Policy,* Vol. I (1940), pp. 3–24; and, more recently, "The Concept of Governmental Responsibility in the United States, Great Britain and the Federal Republic of Germany," a paper presented to the Jablonna Round Table of IPSA (September, 1966). A revised version of the paper, in German, appeared in *Politische Vierteljahrschrift,* Vol. VI (1967).

5. Davis and Hughes, *op. cit.* (note 1 above), p. 40.

6. See my article "Constitution" in the *International Encyclopedia of the Social Sciences* (1967), and the literature cited there, as well as *op. cit.* (note 2, chapter 1), chapters I and VII–IX.

7. Livingston, *op. cit.* (note 3 above), p. 151.

8. Louise Overacker, *The Australian Party System* (1952). In the most recent election, the existing coalition of Liberal and Country Parties was reelected, the two receiving 61 and 21 seats respectively in the House of Representatives, while the opposition Labor Party received 41 seats. See also David B. Truman, *op. cit.* (note 6, chapter 5), especially pp. 128–29.

9. On the general problem of public finance and federalism and, more especially, on the perennial problem of how to divide resources and expenditures, see Friedrich and Baer in Bowie and Friedrich, *op. cit.* (note 1, chapter 1). On Australia in particular, see the comments and work cited in Davis and Hughes, *op. cit.* (note 1 above), pp. 44 ff.

10. For these concluding remarks, compare *Studies in the Australian Constitution,* ed. G. V. Portus (1933), and *Federalism: An Australian Jubilee Study,* ed. G. Sauer (1952). Contra, see Gordon Greenwood, *The Future of Australian Federalism* (1946), who believes it to be a failure.

13

BELGIUM: BREAKUP OF A UNITARY STATE?

BELGIUM PRESENTS, like Canada and Cyprus, a case of intensified conflict between two nationalities which are related to neighboring national states and have been divided by hostile relations over many generations. Its distinctive feature consists in the fact that Belgium has been and is to this day a unitary state built on the principle of bilingualism. This Belgian state is of relatively recent origin. It came into being in 1830, following a revolution against the Netherlands, and was guaranteed its neutrality by an international treaty to which the leading states of Europe were parties. Since the revolution was carried out by the French-speaking Walloons who then, and until recently, constituted a majority, the Belgian constitution of 1831, modeled on French monarchical liberalism and constitutionalism, was given a distinctly unitary and majoritarian character; this despite the Flemish population, which, while alienated from the Dutch (Flemish is a Dutch dialect) by their Catholic religion, possessed a strong sense of identity and formed a distinct cultural community. Eventually this sense of national separateness led to a violent movement for Flemish autonomy, going at times all the way to a demand for independence.[1] As such, this antagonism endangered the very existence of the Belgian state, and in recent years responsible voices could be heard proclaiming that there was no such entity as a Belgian nation. To aggravate the problem, around the turn of the century the Flemish population became the majority and has been inclined to claim for itself the same privileges of predominance which were formerly assumed by the French-speaking Belgians. There are nine provinces altogether, of which the four southern one are French-speaking, while the province of Brabant, which takes in Brussels, is divided; as a result, there is a reasonably clear boundary between the two population groups.

If one keeps Brussels separate—the *Bruxellois* consider themselves as apart—the population balance according to the census of 1948 was: Flemish-speaking, 4,272,392 or 50.19 per cent; French-speaking Walloons, 2,940,543 or 34.54 per cent and *Bruxellois,* 1,298,545 or 15.2 per cent; in short, the Flemish-speaking people have become an absolute majority. At the same time, since the Flemish annual increase through births over deaths is almost seven times that of the Walloons, it has been estimated that the Flemish population will, by 1980, constitute over 60 per cent.[2] It is obvious that this confrontation will aggravate the problems of the French-speaking minority. Some Belgians hope that these problems will have found a federal solution by that time. In the meantime, it is also hoped that Belgium's membership in the European Economic Community as one of the Six will attenuate the sharpness of the clash, since the Netherlands, with whom the Flemish people have—religion apart—a strong cultural and linguistic affinity, is also a member of this more inclusive federal union, and the Benelux countries (Belgium, the Netherlands, and Luxembourg tend to collaborate in facing the much greater power of France and Germany.

Belgium has been a bilingual state since 1898, largely as a

result of the efforts of the Flemish Movement, which came into being soon after the state became independent. To this bilingualism corresponds a bireligionism, since the Catholic preponderance in the country hides the sharp conflict between the clericalism of the conservative Flemish and the liberal anticlericalism of the progressive and socialist Walloons. This contrast is related to the agricultural economy of the North and the mining and industrial economy of the South. Elections have reflected this contrast over many years; at the same time, the interlarding of the party following has served as something of a palliative. In 1958, of the 104 Flemish deputies, 62 were Christian Social, 31 were Socialist, and 10 were Liberals; of the 76 Walloon deputies, on the other hand, 40 were Socialists, 29 were Christian Social, and 5 were Liberals. The Communists were a negligible group. This striking contrast between the Flemish and Walloon parts of the country is, as we said, clearly related to the economic structure; the industrial South has world-wide links which give it a decidedly more cosmopolitan outlook. But this situation is changing, especially since the institution of the EEC. The greater availability of manpower in the North has in fact induced those foreign enterprisers who have come into Belgium to prefer the Flemish part; it is reported that 36 out of 38 foreign firms chose the Flemish section for the establishment of their branches.[3] Furthermore, the French-speaking part of Belgium has been badly hit by the decline of coal mining which has plagued Europe for a number of years. These trends eventually led to the 1960–61 crisis, which was highlighted by strikes and which culminated in demands for constitutional reforms. These reform plans have a considerable history; for the student of federal relationships, they have a good deal of interest, even though none has so far been realized.

In the past, there had been plans to dissolve Belgium, either by joining Flanders (the Flemish part) to Germany, France, or the Netherlands, or by letting it become a separate state.

But these plans have never had substantial support, and so we shall concentrate here upon those plans that aim at maintaining Belgium intact; however, it ought to be remembered that making one or another part into a separate state may become more urgent, if all such moderate solutions fail.

Originally, federal solutions were popular only among the Flemish people, while the Walloons favored decentralization in combination with a parliamentary form akin to Calhoun's idea of "concurrent majorities,"[4] that is, a provision according to which each law had to have the consent of not only a majority of the parliament, but also a majority in each of the two nationality groups.[5] It is odd that such a provision was not recognized as the radically federalistic method that it is and was not seen as the commencement of a federalizing process which its adoption would undoubtedly have engendered.

The plans for federalizing Belgium are, in part at least, based upon Swiss precedent. Favored in the past by the Flemish, they have become the battle-cry of the Walloons since World War II. Spearheaded by the Walloon Movement (originally started in opposition to the Flemish Movement), the Walloon demands are now directed toward establishing a federal state. There has been bitter disagreement over the form of such a state, whether it should be composed of three parts—Flanders, Wallonia, and Brussels—or of two parts (eliminating Brussels), or of the several provinces. It is curious that many advocates of these solutions seem to feel that an autonomous Wallonia would have better chances, economically, than it has now. Presumably it could prevent the application of laws which it considered inimical to its interests, but its promotional appeal would not necessarily increase as a result of such negative action. Politically, the situation would also be aggravated because, on the basis of the distribution of votes indicated above, there would be permanent majorities in both parts, with corresponding acerbation of the relationships between the two. It would seem that a federal system which would retain the present division of provinces would be most likely to function satisfactorily; a reduction to five provinces which has been proposed[6] is undesirable, though better than two or three, and would raise all sorts of problems of redistricting, which are notoriously among the most difficult issues of politics. At the present time, decentralization rather than federalism seems to be the line of compromise.

NOTES TO CHAPTER 13

1. M. P. Herremans, *La Question Flamande* (1948).

2. Herremans, *op. cit.*, p. 54.

3. J. Delacroix, "La Révolte des Modérés ou le Compromis des Belges," *Revue Générale Belge* (1961), pp. 25–36, pleads for toleration and unity; see also, in the same journal, the monthly comments of Memnon (a pseudonym), which are informative and seek to be objective.

4. See John C. Calhoun, *Disquisition on Government* and *Discourse on the Constitution and Government of the United States* (1849–50). See also Chapter 2 of this volume.

5. There is a tendency in Belgium to carry decentralization to the point where it turns into a federalizing process, under the heading of "territorial decentralization"; it is defined as "confier la gestion de *l'ensemble des intérêts régionaux et locaux* des autorités regionales et locales dotées vis-à-vis du pouvoir central de *l'autonomie organique*." In A. Buttgenbach, *Théorie Générale des modes de gestion des services publiques en Belgique* (Brussels, 1952). (Italics in the original.)

6. R. Ullner, "Belgien—Dualismus als Verfassungsprinzip," *Aussenpolitik* (1961), pp. 841 ff. The principle of dualism can, however, hardly be considered an established one; in an authoritative work, such as P. Wigny, *Droit Constitutional* (2 vols., 1952), it plays no significant role.

14

BRAZIL: THE RICH AND THE POOR

BRAZIL PRESENTS a very different federal case, although here, too, economic issues and the retardation of parts of the country have been a key factor in precipitating crisis. But her case is primarily interesting as a demonstration of the limits of federalism as a solution to problems of diversity, when economic conditions are unfavorable. The federal system of Brazil, instituted after the overthrow of the Empire (1889), twice has broken down. The first regime lasted for about four decades but was overthrown, in the sequel of the world economic crisis, in 1934 by Getulio Vargas, who transformed Brazil into a dictatorship on the fascist model (Estado Novo).[1] Re-established in 1946, the second federal model did not last two decades, although its outward forms, retained by the military dictatorship, may be considered a continuation. It should be noted in this connection that Brazilian scholars have been inclined to question the federal nature of Brazil after 1946,[2] but since these arguments were mostly based on an outworn static and formalistic conception of federalism, they need not detain us here. In any case, Brazil was, in 1946, reconstituted as a closely integrated federal order, comparable to India (see chapter 18).

The Brazilian social structure is characterized by extremes of contrast between classes and regions. Enormous wealth in São Paulo and Rio de Janeiro contrasts with abject poverty and a very low standard of living in the North and West of the country. São Paulo, with 18 per cent of the population, produces 55 per cent of the country's industrial goods and receives over one-third of the national income. It stands to reason that São Paulo and the three other leading states (there are 21) should tend to control the national government; yet its tasks have primarily been those connected with the need for economic development in the poorer states.

What was said concerning the first republic's federalism applies *caeteris paribus* to the second: "Federalism and republicanism, instead of consolidating the country and creating the consciousness of a Brazilian nationhood, only helped to paralyze the solidarity of the people and to promote a vicious regionalism in which the two most powerful states, São Paulo and Minas Gerais, dominated for their own economic and political interests the whole country."[3] And yet, the second form of federalism had given so much power to the center that it could even be questioned whether it was, properly speaking, in accord with the federal principle. As one Brazilian constitutional lawyer put it, the states were free only to elect their governors and deputies to the state assembly.[4] "As one reads the text of the Constitution of 1946, one is struck so forcibly by the overwhelming scope of the Union's jurisdiction as to wonder what could possibly be left to the states," an outside observer has added.[5] It seems more than doubtful that such arguments, based upon formalistic criteria of competency, constitute a realistic assessment; even in 1961, the states and communes in Brazil together only had slightly more revenue than the federal government—for the federal government, 308 billion cruzeiros, as against 308 billion for the states and 62 billion for the communes.[6] In the vigorous federal system of the United States, as well as in Switzerland, the Federal Republic of Germany, and elsewhere, the federal authorities collect a much larger percentage of the total revenue. In the United States, the total revenue figures for 1962, in millions of dollars, were: Federal: $106,441; State: $37,597; Local: $43,278.[7]

It does not seem realistic, therefore, to blame the increase in federal activity for the breakdown of Brazilian federalism, or to insist contrariwise that this federalism was a disguised unitary state, as Vargas' regime had been. It seems much more nearly correct to suggest that the federal authorities had failed to satisfy the country's economic needs and had therefore yielded to radical, even Communist elements. And that argument brings us back to the disparity between the states. In every federal system some of the component units will be more opulent than others: New York is richer than Mississippi, Zurich more so than Unterwalden, Rhineland-Westphalia with its Ruhr decidedly more so than Schleswig-Holstein. Indeed, it might be said that these very contrasts are part of the federal bargain. But they are only bearable, and that is to say politically durable, if the federal authorities are intent upon balancing the imbalance by federal subsidies in one form or another. In the United States, the contribution in the form of grants-in-aid in one of the poorer states, Wyoming, during the late 1950's was over $50 per capita while the contribution of the states' citizens (by way of federal income tax) was less than $200 per capita. But these contrasts are much more extreme in the case of Brazil. States like Guanabara (Rio de Janeiro) and São Paulo are modern communities on the standard of the West, while in the northern and western sections of Brazil, conditions are as poor as in the most underdeveloped parts of Latin America and Asia. The per capita income is as low as $100, and many of these "states" can operate modern facilities and attempt to effect some development

only by means of federal support. Hence the federal government is called upon to redistribute income and to manage the
economic growth of the poorer regions. In this task it has not
succeeded, and the measures needed for accomplishing significant results aroused the antagonism which ultimately un-
dermined the regime.

In view of this situation, it does not make much sense to
argue that autonomy will be sacrificed to the central government. Nor can such floundering policies as the federal government of Brazil has promoted—and which have resulted in
inflation and a breakdown of the external balance of pay-
ments—be usefully described as an "economic dictatorship
over the states."[8] Rather, the conclusion which seems to impose itself is that federalism is no cure for inadequate, not to
say incompetent, government. Indeed, it requires a high degree of skill and the pragmatic capacity for compromise. But
neither is a unitary state such a solution. Just as the Weimar
Republic did not fail *because* of its weak federal structure, so
Brazil did not do so, though there are striking parallels between the centralistic federalism of both. Brazilian federalism
suffers from the fact that it is not an institutional outgrowth
of its own peculiar social realities, as are the federalisms of
Switzerland, the United States, and the Federal Republic of
Germany. In the case of Brazil, federalism was artificially imposed upon a country that had lived under a unitary monarchy. Its institutions were largely copied from the United
States Constitution without Brazil in any real sense resembling
the American reality of 1787 or later. "A unitary state, which
had worked well for two generations, was broken up into
artificial segments which were endowed with political independence without being ripe for it or even desiring it," Karl
Loewenstein has written.[9] Since only a few of the country's
states have a cultural or economic personality of their own,
being the successors to colonial districts, the rest cannot hope
and do not desire to maintain themselves as states. In view of

the large size and the wide diversities of the country, a radical decentralization would seem a more sensible constitutional program than a federal system. Perhaps something like the unitary federal state could be made to work.[10]

NOTES TO CHAPTER 14

1. Karl Loewenstein, *Brazil Under Vargas* (1942), especially pp. 9 ff. and 59 ff. On the first republic, see J. G. James, *The Constitutional System of Brazil* (1923), *passim*.

2. "Perspectivas do Federalismo Brasileiro," a special issue of *Revista Brasileira de Estudos Politicos* (1958).

3. This summary is found in Loewenstein, *op. cit.*, p. 14. He himself is critical of this outlook, but thinks rather that "the federal principle was driven to unhealthy extremes." He believes that the attack on federalism served as a foil for antidemocratic sentiments.

4. G. de Britto Mello Boson, in *op. cit.* (note 2 above), p. 72. See also on this Leslie Lipson, "The Federal Principle and the Brazilian Reality," *Public Policy*, Vol. XIV (1965), pp. 444–55. This paper is based on a report to IPSA (Geneva Congress, 1964).

5. Lipson, *op. cit.*, p. 5.

6. Lipson, *op. cit.*, p. 6, and *Annuario Estatístico* (1963). The statistics which Lipson quotes do not prove his point, as they could easily be duplicated elsewhere; for example, consider the amount of federal income tax coming in from New York, Pennsylvania, and California.

7. *Statistical Abstract of the United States* (Bureau of the Census, U.S. Department of Commerce: 1964). It should be remembered, however, that the figures would contrast less strongly if allowance were made for the huge military expenditures of the U.S. federal government.

8. J. Pinto Antunes, "O Principio Federative na Costituiçao Brasileira," *Revista da Faculdado de Direito* (Gérais, 1953). Lipson cites this statement with approval, but it seems to me obscure, if not meaningless.

9. Loewenstein, *op. cit.*, p. 13. See also his description of the imbalance, p. 74.

10. See chapter 23 of this volume, where Konrad Hesse, *Der Unitarische Bundesstaat* (1962) is discussed. Soviet federalism certainly fits this pattern; see Klaus von Beyme, *op. cit.* (note 1, chapter 5).

15

CANADA: CULTURAL CONFLICT AND FEDERAL FAILURE?

THE CANADIAN FEDERAL RELATIONSHIP, long believed to be a very stable compromise,[1] has in recent years become the subject of violent controversy. An insistent demand for independence on the part of a substantial group of the French Canadians has precipitated a crisis of major proportions. It is a striking case of the disruptive force of nationalism and linguistic separatism. As a Royal Commission put it recently: "Indeed it seemed [from the testimony taken] that French-speaking participants used the term 'nation' to emphasize their understanding of a binational Canada, while English-speaking ones used it to insist on the necessity of 'national unity' for the country."[2] This misunderstanding between English-speaking and French-speaking Canadians regarding the meaning of the very term "nation" is symptomatic of this conflict. It cannot be explained away by reference to the meaning of *nation* in French—on the contrary, French usage inclines to link the concept of *nation* to that of *État*.[3]

During the testimony taken by the aforementioned Royal Commission, many spoke of the fact that other nationalities, besides the French, had become assimilated. Why not the French? The answer must be given in terms of numbers, compactness of settlement, and complete predominance in one province—Quebec. There can be little question that such concentration and recognition within the federal framework makes a vital difference. Bilingualism is both the cause and the reinforced result of such an arrangement. There is an old legend that German almost became the official language of the state of Pennsylvania, and that it took the persuasive power of Benjamin Franklin to prevent it. No one knows, of course, what might have been the consequence; there can be no doubt that it would have strengthened German separatism.[4] In a sense, therefore, we may state at least hypothetically that federal recognition of a nationality and its language reinforces its differential development and hence centrifugal tendencies. In light of the Swiss experience, it may be doubted, however, that this need be the result, if the two or more language groups are placed on a basis of strict equality. What has caused the trouble in Canada is the attitude of bland superiority expressed by many English-speaking Canadians: If English is the majority's language, then that alone is what we will speak. In this connection, it is worth observing that the confrontation of two languages, one of the majority and the other of the minority, seems to be particularly prone to precipitate conflict. Bilingualism may be linguistically more manageable than multilingualism, but it is also politically more difficult to cope with (see also chapters 13 and 16).

A little over 30 per cent of Canada's total population of 18,233,247 are of French ethnic origin, while not quite 44 per cent are British; so, the balance is not quite a third against not quite a half. Over four-fifths of the French-speaking Canadians are concentrated in the Province of Quebec, where they constitute over four-fifths of the total population of the province (4,241,354 out of 5,259,211). The rest are scattered widely and, except in New Brunswick (38.82 per cent), nowhere reach anything near the national percentage figure. There is a rapid dropping off toward the West, with Ontario—the province with the largest population (6,236,092)—having just over 10 per cent Canadians of French ethnic origin.[5] Since the third largest ethnic element are the Germans, who make up not quite 6 per cent and whose percentage increases toward the West, it is clear that the Anglo-French conflict is the decisive one. The other nationalities tend, as is usual in such situations, to side and assimilate with the English-speaking elements, though when taken together they could give a majority to the opposition.

These ethnic figures are somewhat misleading. If one considers mother tongue, English speakers appear to be nearly 60 per cent, whereas the French contingent does not quite constitute 30 per cent; and if "official language" is considered, there are over 67 per cent who report "only English," while a mere 19 per cent report "only French," with a significant 12 per cent claiming both languages, thus showing that about a third of the French-speaking population are bilingual, against perhaps 3 per cent of the rest of the people. This kind of imbalance contrasts sharply with the Swiss situation (see chapter 20), where bilingualism is widespread. But the basic pattern is the same: In the case of Canada, a large English-speaking majority outside the Province of Quebec, and a large French-speaking majority in Quebec. As the Royal Commission Report points out, the chief protagonists are French-speaking Quebec and English-speaking Canada; it is a conflict between two majorities. Quebec wants and is building itself into an autonomous society.

The development of this determination to recapture its cultural identity and to reinforce it by the formation of an autonomous state rests upon many factors. The clash is based upon ancient enmities. But it is reinforced by economic disparities, especially in industrial control and per capita income. Yet central to the Canadian situation is the dualism of two cultures. Canadian federalism, according to some Canadian theorists, rests upon an implicit compact between or alliance of these two cultures.[6] It is difficult to see how such a theory can be combined with the highly centralistic tenor of the British North America Act (1867). Rather, the Canadian situation would seem to correspond to the theory of the unitary federal state, though here it is not the creation of the constituent people themselves, but rather the "mother country." This may in fact be part of the difficulties.

In a long series of interpretative decisions, the Privy Council, until recently the Court of last resort, strengthened the power of the states, thus responding to the realities of Canadian dualism; this judicial federalizing process has, however, been sharply criticized.[7] It certainly ran counter to the trend in the United States, so that a critic could write that where a "looser federalism in the United States was unified by the judgments of a Marshall, in Canada a stronger union was decentralized by a Watson and a Haldane."[8] But this phase came to an end in this century, when Canadian independence from the control of the British parliament had been completed. The rising tide of economic direction, common to so many countries, led to a rapid extension of federal activity, promoted by political leadership. There can be little question that this increase in central activity and power served to exacerbate the situation of the French Canadians and was thus bound to intensify their desire for greater autonomy, even at the risk of some economic disadvantage. Cooperative federalism has been of some help in this connection, as it has in other federal systems, but the actual imbalance is so pronounced that cooperation is difficult. It is probably true that it strengthens both levels of government, and is not merely a cloak for centralism, but it does not provide the degree of local autonomy which the French Canadians desire. They do not wish to become "dignified and haughty pensioners rather than partners of the national government."[9] On the contrary, they insist upon the partnership becoming real.

The resistance to the spreading power of the federal government is not limited to Quebec and the French Canadians. It is also increasingly felt in Ontario and British Columbia.[10] Especially where taxes and public expenditure are concerned, these provinces wish to extend rather than curtail provincial autonomy. But the hard core of the fight for expanding such autonomy is undoubtedly Quebec. In essence, as one author has said of the French Canadians, "they do not wish to be treated as outsiders [yet] they want to remain a separate group."[11] The same author reported that one of Quebec's top public servants, Claude Morin, told him: "Every French Canadian is at heart a separatist." But it is not only the question of federal power; it is also that of local control.[12] In keeping with such sentiments, the government of Quebec has been developing a vigorous program of industrial conquest, that is to say a program under which the effective control and management of business and industry in Quebec would be in French-Canadian hands. Using hydroelectric power, banking, and steel as starting points, the government of Premier Daniel Johnson has already achieved vital progress in the direction of such a conquest. As a part of it, Johnson has wrested nearly 50 per cent of the income tax revenue from the federal authorities, as against the 18 per cent the provinces normally have been getting.

Canadian federalism has been evolving at such a rapid rate, and, especially, the federal relationship of Quebec has undergone so extensive an evolution, that it seems difficult to delineate future developments. When both the federal and the Quebec governments have already authorized a study of the possible consequences of complete separation and when at least one premier of a western province has declared that he would propose his province's joining the United States in case of the secession of Quebec, it is obvious that something dramatic will be needed to institutionalize the distinct relationship of Quebec to the rest of the country. Perhaps the Canadian Premiers' Conference, which was established in

1960, can be developed to provide a new symbol of provincial autonomy; perhaps the conventional representation of distinct provinces in the federal cabinet could be constitutionally firmed to provide a recognition of the dualism that is Canada's cultural reality. But to an outside observer, the Royal Commission was wise when it reminded its readers of Lord Durham's remark, in his famous report of 1839: "I found two nations warring in the bosom of a single state." They rightly add that the present crisis concerns the totality of two societies, and they remind us that such a relationship, "like anything that is living, must constantly adapt to changing conditions."[13]

NOTES TO CHAPTER 15

1. See Bowie and Friedrich, *op. cit.* (note 1, chapter 1), which contains specific sections on all the topics of Canadian federal relationships. Its bibliography is superseded by the excellent contribution of Alexander Brady to Livingston, *op. cit.* (note 4, chapter 10), pp. 11–28. See also Taylor Cole, *op. cit.* (note 4, chapter 10).

2. *Royal Commission Report, op. cit.* (note 7, chapter 3), p. 48. This report speaks of "crisis," pp. 133 ff.

3. R. Johannet, *Le Principe des nationalités* (new ed., 1927); see also my discussion in my *op. cit.* (note 1, chapter 1), chapters 29 and 30.

4. John A. Hawgood, *The Tragedy of German-America* (1940), p. 93, remarks that the massing of German immigrants in Pennsylvania "did not result from any deliberate attempt to found a New Germany. . . ."; he adds that "the Pennsylvania Dutch [were] not interested and did not participate in the efforts . . . to found a true 'New Germany' or a series of New Germanies in America that were made in the nineteenth century." Such attempts were made in Missouri (Hawgood, chapter V) and in Texas (Hawgood, chapter VI).

5. *Royal Commission Report, op. cit.* (note 7, chapter 3), Appendix V, pp. 190 ff.

6. Alexander Brady, in Livingston, *op. cit.* (note 4, chapter 10); the particular issue is treated on pp. 13 ff. See also the *Trembley Report* (4 vols., 1956).

7. Taylor Cole, *op. cit.* (note 4, chapter 10), discusses this matter critically, citing Frank R. Scott's view, as offered "French-Canada and Canadian Federalism," in A. R. M. Lower and others, *Evolving Canadian Federalism* (1958). See Lower himself, p. 40.

8. Frank R. Scott, "Centralization and Decentralization in Canadian Federalism," *Canadian Bar Review*, Vol. 29 (1951), p. 1104, as cited by Cole.

9. J. A. Corry, in Lower, *op. cit.* (note 7 above), p. 124.

10. See footnotes 27 and 28 in Cole, *op. cit.* (note 4, chapter 10).

11. Philip Siekman, *Fortune*, 1964.

12. The facts support the French-Canadian sentiments, at least in part.

Until quite recently, the control of banking, industry, and commerce was largely concentrated in the hands of Anglo-Canadians, even in Quebec Province. Also, there was widespread prejudice against French Canadians when it came to employment and advancement opportunities, especially in the financial-industrial complex.

13. *Royal Commission Report, op. cit.* (note 7, chapter 3), p. 144.

16

CYPRUS: THE DANGERS OF DUALISM

THE FEDERAL ORDER OF CYPRUS provides the clearest case for the argument that federalism is ill-suited to situations in which the will to federal cooperation (common values, interests, and beliefs) is weak, especially when only two partners exist, of whom one constitutes a clear majority. The difficulties are compounded when both elements in the community are related to interested outside powers which themselves are in conflict.[1] That is precisely the situation of Cyprus. Cyprus is a large island (3,572 sq. miles) in the eastern Mediterranean; it lies within sight of the Asiatic coast, opposite Lebanon and Turkey. Its population level, which increases rapidly (by about 1.75 per cent per year), is about 600,000, of which 18 per cent are Turks, while the largest part of the remainder (77 per cent) are Greeks. Most of the latter are native to the island, while the Turks are descendants of a population settled in Cyprus during the Ottoman rule that began in the seventeenth and ended in the nineteenth century. Britain acquired Cyprus as recently as 1878. In 1960, independence was granted. In this connection, a treaty was concluded between

Great Britain, Greece, Turkey, and the Republic of Cyprus (August 16, 1960). At the same time, a constitution came into force; it had been drafted by a Joint Commission upon the basis of an agreement, resulting from conferences at Zurich and London in 1959, which became known as the Cyprus Agreement. This agreement, and the constitution derived from it, sought to bridge the deep gulf which divided the Greek and Turkish Cypriotes by an elaborate dualism. The gulf is the result of the historic animosity of the two peoples, dating back to the Turkish conquest and the Greek struggle for liberation. It is deepened by differences of religion, language, and many related aspects of culture. Since Greeks and Turks are separated to an extent, but not living in geographically well-defined areas (though there are great differences in density of distribution and plans have been on foot for complete separation), the federalism chosen for Cyprus was what might be called "corporate federalism"—a scheme once proposed for the solution of the nationality problems of the Hapsburg Empire and afterward adopted in Estonia.[2] Federalism there was based on a nonterritorial plan whereunder a person could choose which particular nationality he wished to belong to and participate in. It is not clear from the record whether the Austrian plan or the Estonian experience had any influence upon the constitution makers for Cyprus. In any case they structured their federal scheme upon a comparable idea, as generally the constitution of Cyprus follows the continental European rather than British or American precedent.[3]

The federal bargain, in the case of Cyprus, was very carefully worked out in terms of what appears to have been an unresolved conflict. It was forcefully supported by the Greek Cypriotes, who were led by the strong and wily Archbishop Makarios, the Ethnarch, or ruler, of his people. Resisted by the Turkish minority to the very end, the compromise which the British accepted did not rest upon a deep-seated will to unity, except among a part of the majority.⁴ As a result, the existing dualism was recognized throughout the constitution and became a built-in part of it. Its extremely long and complicated provisions constitute an elaborate scheme of checks and balances, in which the need for organizing the community for effective action is sacrificed to the purpose of preventing the abuse of power by one of the two parties to the bargain. Right at the start, there is provision for a president who must be a Greek and a vice-president who must be a Turk. It was not long before the two, instead of cooperating, were at loggerheads; since they did not owe their election to one constituency, but were the representatives of the two nationalities —the Greeks electing the president, and the Turks the vice-president—this was hardly to be wondered at. There follow provisions for two official languages, for flying the flags of the two nations along with that of Cyprus, and for celebrating the respective national holidays.

The basic error of having two chief executives, representing the two hostile communities, was continued downward in the governmental hierarchy. The cabinet, or Council of Ministers, was made up of ten members; seven were to be Greeks and three were to be Turks, named respectively by the president and vice-president; yet decisions were to be taken by majority, so that the Greeks could—and did—disregard the Turks. Likewise, there was to be a dualism in other top offices, such as the Attorney General. Again, the entire civil service was to be composed 70 per cent of Greeks and 30 per cent of Turks, with as much matching as possible throughout. A surer recipe for failure to achieve a working federal bargain could hardly be imagined. The federalizing process, which is the crux of a working federal order, could not possibly get under way in such conditions.

But the error was compounded by the legislative setup. There was provided a House of Representatives of fifty members: thirty-five Greeks and fifteen Turks. This House had a president who was a Greek elected by the Greeks and a Turkish vice-president to be elected by the Turks. But even this degree of dualistic splintering of the legislative power was not deemed adequate. So, in addition, Communal Chambers were organized to be in charge of legislation in regard to religion, education, culture, and family and personal relations, and were even given their own separate taxing power in order "to provide for the community's needs." (See the Yugoslav "chambers," chapter 22.) These Communal Chambers were each elected by their respective national community and therefore in a sense corresponded to the legislatures of territorial subdivisions in classical federal systems. But since they possessed no clearly assigned executive establishment, they were bound to act as a disruptive element in reinforcing the divisive tendencies in the dualistically-structured civil service.

As if these provisions, which organized only conflict and competition and omitted all institutional safeguards for cooperation, were not enough to doom the federal relationship, it was further provided that the relationship of each of the two nationalities to their outside national communities should be reinforced by such arrangements as subsidies from the Greek and Turkish governments for education and the like, and by the participation of clergymen, professors, and teachers from Greece and Turkey.

So radical a system of divided power and conflicting competencies desperately needed an umpire in the form of a constitutional court to adjudicate differences regarding the interpretation of these provisions. But how could one find a neutral arbiter? The Supreme Constitutional Court as well as the Supreme Judicial Court were both composed in the same dualistic fashion by one Greek and one Turkish judge, with an outsider as third member and president of the court. Actually, one of these outsiders was a German, the other a Canadian. In the Constitutional Court the president tried to cope with the situation by persuading his colleagues not to render any decisions, except unanimously; the result was, of course, that no decisions could be rendered on matters in controversy between Greeks and Turks, although these were the only matters calling for decision under the circumstances. Eventually, the president resigned, because the Greek President of the Republic brought heavy pressure upon him to side with the Greek member in making a decision. Similarly, the president of the Supreme Judicial Court resigned.

The stumbling bloc proved to be the management of local government; the Greeks sought to make it more effectively operative by providing for unified rather than dualistic control. The Turks considered this a clear violation of both the letter and the spirit of the constitution. Presumably they were right (we do not wish to enter into the elaborate formalistic arguments) and the president of the court inclined to render that kind of formalistically correct judgment.[5] But constitutions are not formal documents; they must be interpreted flexibly to allow for the developing social context, as the history of the U.S. Supreme Court shows very clearly. It may be doubted, however, whether a constitution so ill-constructed and embodying so incomplete a federal bargain could have been made to work by any judge, no matter how wise.

The lesson of the Cyprus experiment—and it is an important one—is that a federal system requires for its effective functioning adequate machinery for continuous readjustment. There must exist workable institutional devices, "mechanisms," if you please, for reassessing the position and for allowing the partners to negotiate further bargains to implement the existing one. In short, the structure must allow the federalizing process to go forward. But no machinery, no matter how skillfully contrived, can serve effectively if it is not supported by a determined will to make it work—if there is no commitment to a degree of federal unity as well as the determination to maintain local values, interests, and beliefs intact. A dual regime compounded of two hostile groups, one bent on domination and majority rule, the other preferring separation and secession provides no foundation for the operation of the difficult system that is federalism.

NOTES TO CHAPTER 16

1. *Cyprus* (H.M. Statistical Office, 1960) contains the agreements, constitutions, and other important material. The sketch which follows is replete with data drawn from this important source. An interesting supplementary study is A. J. Meyer (with Simos Vassiliou), *The Economy of Cyprus* (1962), which I found very useful.

2. Karl Renner, *Der Kampf der Österreichischen Nationen um den Staat* (1907), and the same author's *Das Selbstbestimmungsrecht der Nationen* (1918). For Estonia, see Evald Uustalu, *The History of the Estonian People* (1952). The whole issue is related to Héraud's thought, *op. cit.* (note 1, chapter 4).

3. McWhinney, *op. cit.* (note 6, chapter 3), pp. 64 ff.

4. Stanley Mayes, *Cyprus and Makarios* (1960), especially chapters 8–11, is sharply critical of the Cypriote leader; Sir Harry Luke, *Cyprus* (1957), is a lively, if uncritically pro-British account; see also Treaty Concerning the Establishment of the Republic of Cyprus, Nicosia, August 16, 1960. (Cmnd. 1252, 1962).

5. Ernst Forsthoff, the German Chief Justice of the Supreme Court of Cyprus until 1964, has offered his rather formalistic notions on constitutional interpretation in *Zur Problematik der Verfassungsauslegung* (1961). Had Marshall and other U.S. Supreme Court Justices followed such norms, the U.S. Constitution could never have evolved in the way that it has.

17

GERMANY: DELEGATED ADMINISTRATION AT WORK

THE CASE OF GERMANY, or rather of the Federal Republic of Germany, is particularly interesting from the viewpoint of federal administration. For here the system of delegated administration is developed to a very high degree. It has a long tradition and is linked to the strong sense of local patriotism which has been characteristic of Germany throughout most of her history. Leaving aside the medieval period and the earlier modern times when Germany was divided into many principalities, we find that after her unification in the Empire, in 1871, delegated administration became the rule for a large part of federal administration. This was due to the fact that the large principalities, such as the kingdoms of Bavaria, Württemberg, and Saxony, not to speak of Prussia, had highly developed administrative services[1] which had been in charge of the execution of local law. As such laws were gradually replaced by federal legislation, it seemed the better part of wisdom to allow the existing services to carry on, and indeed, through the Federal Council, to participate in the shaping of federal legislation. Under the Weimar Republic, after 1919, this tradition was partially abandoned, and a number of federal (*reichseigene*) administrations were organized; their top-heavy bureaucracy became one of the controversial features of that ill-fated system. Hitler's radical concentration of all power, both legislative and administrative, caused not only a strong demand for a return to federal relationships between Germany's constituent parts, but also a natural reaction in favor of its tradition of delegated administration. The fact that such delegated administration was also practiced in Switzerland suggested that it was not "undemocratic" to resume it.[2]

The constitutional provisions for delegated administration are embodied in Title VIII of the Basic Law (Constitution) of the Federal Republic, comprising Articles 83–91.[3] They are of considerable complexity. The foreign service, the federal finance administration (internal revenue), the federal bank, the railroads, the postal service, waterways and shipping, social insurance, armed forces, and, finally, air transport are designated as part of federal administration proper. Most other matters forming the subject of some federal legislation are administered by the *Länder* (states) under federal supervision. Thus federal policy is executed by the *Länder* governments who administer these matters as "of their own concern" —that is to say, as if these were the results of their own policy—establishing the necessary offices and issuing the needed rules and regulations. At the same time, the federal government may issue general rules, which are, however, subject to approval by the Federal Council. This means in practice that the administrations of the *Länder* governments, acting in the Federal Council by a majority of votes (21 out of 41), must be willing to accept such a general regulation; they often are.[4]

In exercising its supervision, the federal government may send commissioners to a *Land* government, and if the Minister President of the *Land* government refuses access to the

Land authorities concerned, the federal government can go to the Federal Council and seek authorization for approaching the particular *Land* authorities directly. In general, this supervision, which also involves the making of reports and the submission of documents, functions smoothly; the cases where conflict has resulted are relatively rare. The federal authorities may and do request that shortcomings be corrected. But what happens if they are not and conflict results? The Basic Law provides that in such cases the Federal Council is to be the umpire. It decides, upon application of the federal government, who is right, and if this does not settle the matter, it may be appealed to the Constitutional Court. The court has had to handle some cases, but not very many.[5]

The federal government may also issue instructions to the *Land* authorities and, if it can secure the assent of the Federal Council, it may issue "individual instructions for particular cases." Unless the matter is urgent, such instructions must, like all instructions, be addressed to the "highest *Land* authorities," that is to say, the Minister President. Here again we see the careful effort to protect as far as possible *Land* autonomy against federal interference in local administration. On the other hand, so intimate a matter as the training of civil servants was given to the federal government to regulate, and it has done so. This arrangement has resulted in a certain rigidity and has served to buttress the near-monopolizing of the civil service by the legal profession (*Juristenmonopol*).[6]

If it be asked what is the standard or criteria by which federal supervision is exercised, the answer is found in the Basic Law, which says that supervision may not only be in terms of conformity with the law, but also in terms of the appropriateness of the execution, at least where the *Land* operates by mandate of the federal government. In other words, the effectiveness of what the *Land* authorities undertake in the course of administering federal law is part of the supervision. A fairly elaborate code of regulations has been developed to further circumscribe the actual procedures. More detailed provisions are made with regard to the armed forces in case the federal government should call upon the *Länder* to act as "agents" of the federal authorities in order to give the federal authorities a greater degree of power and free them of the necessity of securing the consent of the Federal Council. Special provisions are also made for the administration of federal highways and motor roads by the *Länder*.

This entire system, as envisaged in the constitution, has been greatly altered and implemented by the further delegation of the execution and administration of federal legislation to the cities (*Städte*) and counties (*Landkreise*), that is, to the communes (municipal corporations). The administration of cities is rather autonomous and separate from the state administration, while the administration of the counties is intertwined with that of the states, but has also become increasingly autonomous. Hence the administration of both state and federal legislation is carried out by the local bodies which are administering the two kinds of law together. Nor do they form special administrative units; rather, their administration is organized according to functions and these functional departments administer federal, state, and local law jointly. In effect they integrate all administration.

The resulting separation of policy formation and execution brings it about that the control turns upon the principle of "legality" (*Gesetzmaessigkeit*), which in turn leads to stating the policy in great detail in the form of normative law. That is the reason why German administration is to such a large extent handled by men trained in the law—the abovementioned monopoly of the jurists. For such legally trained civil servants possess the capacity to interpret and apply the legal norms which are handed them by the superior authorities. They are further encouraged to do so by their subjection to the very active practice of administrative courts. These administrative courts provide a large part of the control. All this judicial supervision is integrated on the national level by the Federal Administrative Court; similar State Administrative Courts integrate the local activities. In order that such a system function effectively, it is necessary that the citizen is ready and willing to appeal to the administrative courts, whenever he feels that the administrative authorities step outside the law. Germans are notoriously willing to do so, and are encouraged by the rather simple procedure and by the inclination of these courts to favor the citizen rather than the administrator. Thus a good deal of the control which might be difficult internally is provided by external judicial control.

Such a system would not work unless the officials were interested in the judicial decisions. In fact, the bureaucrats are keenly concerned, since any decision against their work carries the implication of illegality. The often-belabored "legalism" of German administration is rooted in this attention of the German official to judicial precedents, which in turn reinforces the "monopoly of the jurists." Without being trained in law, it is difficult to be a good administrator under such a system. As a consequence, the superior *Land* and federal authorities need not be too much concerned with controlling the execution of federal law. A further advantage of this system is that such a legally-controlled administration does not have to organize new offices for each new task. The *Land* authorities hand on to the cities and counties the new legislation, which simply requires the department in charge to handle the matter; the department is enlarged rather than having a new agency instituted, and the problems of supervision and control remain the same.[7]

One important administrative means of supervision and control is the tradition of requiring reports, which in turn becomes the basis of communications, including instructions (*Anordnungen*) and orders (*Erlasse*). But these communications also usually take the form of general norms rather than being specific and addressed to a particular office or official.

Where administration operates freely and according to discretion rather than legal norm, the federal influence is wielded by means of grants-in-aid, with specific conditions attached, as in road-building and other public works. The techniques, familiar in the United States, are reasonably effective in securing the quality of the performance.[8]

NOTES TO CHAPTER 17

1. For the concept of a developed bureaucracy, see my *op. cit.* (note 2, chapter 4), chapter II.

2. For what follows, see Bowie and Friedrich, *Studies in Federalism* (1954), pp. 93 ff. and the literature cited there.

3. For the translation of the text, see William G. Andrews, *Constitutions and Constitutionalism* (2d ed., 1963), pp. 125–29.

4. For this and other concrete detail, see Karl-Heinz Neunreither, "Politics and Bureaucracy in the West German Bundesrat," *American Political Science Review*, LIII (1959), pp. 713 ff.

5. Edward McWhinney, *Constitutionalism in Germany and the Federal Constitutional Court* (1962); Taylor Cole, "The West German Federal Constitutional Court: An Evaluation," *Journal of Politics*, Vol. 20 (1958), pp. 278 ff.

6. See Ralph Dahrendorf, *Gesellschaft und Demokratie in Deutschland* (1966), chapter 16.

7. See authors cited in note 6, chapter 8.

8. Article 120(a) of the Basic Law; note the commentary to the *Lastenausgleichsgesetz* by Rudolf Harmening (1953 and many later editions).

18

INDIA: FEDERALISM AND CULTURAL DIVERSIFICATION

INDIA'S FEDERAL EXPERIMENT is particularly interesting, because of its increasing differentiation, due to the diversity in languages and economic development. While originally it was hoped by its creators that India would become monolingual in the course of a few years, it has actually proven necessary not only to accept multilingualism, but also to restructure the country's effective divisions in accordance with diversified cultural and linguistic ambitions. It might be objected here that the issues India presents are not, properly speaking, related to federalism, since many Indian scholars insist that India is not a federal system, but "a unitary state with subsidiary federal features."[1] But apart from the fact that such arguments are usually based on too narrow a conception of federalism, excluding the "unitary federal state" (see chapter 23), India is clearly undergoing a federalizing process in the course of which federal diversity is increasing. It is, as has been shown a number of times in this study, a recurrent feature of this process that in the course of the democratizing of a society, regional and linguistic-cultural communities become more articulate and demand recognition in the form of a set of political institutions, including safeguards for the identity of the particular community. India is as much a case in point as Belgium, Canada, Cyprus, and the rest.

It stands to reason that, at first, after independence had been won and British imperial rule had been replaced by local authority, unitary sentiment should have been very strong—especially after one of the major subdivisions, namely the Moslem community, had broken away into a separate Pakistan. Yet, even though the federal scheme of the Constitution of 1935 had proved unworkable, there was virtually no sentiment for the establishment of a constitutionally unitary state;[2] but there was powerful sentiment for giving the central authorities sufficient power to combat the centrifugal tendencies in so vast a country with so rich a diversity of cultures, languages, and religions, and it is submitted that the extent of these formal powers cannot be made the measuring rod of the force of regionalism and federalism in India. The consolidation and regrouping of the original subdivisions—largely the result of dynastic conquest in the princely states and of British administrative expediency in the rest of India —into fairly large units of unilingual homogeneity has increased the weight of the states considerably.[3] As a leading Indian scholar put it recently: "It would be rash to assume that the federal system in India has definitely settled down to the acceptance of central dominance. The growth of regional consciousness has only just begun and new problems based on it are coming to the surface despite the weight of law, custom and habit on the side of the Center."[4]

Among the most interesting challenges to centralizing tendencies and the former unitary propensity is the opposition to policies designed to carry out the constitutional injunction for establishing Hindi as the common language of India; such terms as "Hindi imperialism" are at times heard in the course of such opposition.[5] Planning, the distribution of revenues, and related issues of economic policy add to the opposition's ammunition. Hence the federalizing tendency is on the increase.

The linguistic factor in the Indian federalizing process deserves some further analysis, especially since it is a multilingual pattern, but one in which *each* language tends to be identified with *one* state. This holds, of course, only for the major languages; many minor ones must be and are to some extent protected by the central government, as provided in the constitution (Article 350A). How, in such a situation a common language can be established is as yet an unsolved problem.[6] The selection of Hindi is understandable in terms of the politics of the Congress Party, many of whose leaders came from the section of the country, including Delhi, in which Hindi is the common speech. But according to the best testimony, the foremost literary language of India is Bengali; Tamil has a very long literary tradition; Sanskrit is the vehicle of the ancient epic and great religious literature; hence each of these has a better claim to prestige and respect. "Objective and weighty criteria tend to rank it [Hindi] below at least Sanskrit, Tamil and Bengali,"[7] we hear, and there is violent resentment spreading against the "imposition" of an inferior and rather recent language (Hindi emerged during the last 100 years). It is rightly claimed that the prestige of a language is associated with its literature, and Hindi lacks such prestige because of its ordinary, lowbrow character. As a leading Indian scholar put it in 1959: "The new Hindi, as it continues to develop, is not a language, but a burlesque."[8]

As a result, English continues as the available *lingua franca* of a good part of the governing and business elite of India, subject to the qualification that the rising local politicians, as noted above, are more and more inclined to communicate in their own idiom with their mass following. This is only natural, considering that democratic party politics has to be carried on at the grass roots and, hence, will also turn to local habits of speech that can be readily understood by, and generally appeal to, the common folk, the mass electorate. No matter how much an intellectual elite may dislike it, the lower-caste leaders, rising rapidly in the democratic context of modern India, will follow the path of least linguistic resistance. A manifestation of this trend was apparent in the election of 1967.[9]

The Indian constitution recognizes fourteen languages, besides English: Assamese, Bengali, Gujarati, Hindi, Kannada, Kashmiri, Malayalam, Marathi, Oriya, Panjabi, Sanskrit, Tamil, Telegu, and Urdu (Article 351). As each of these languages is spoken by many millions, it proved possible to reorganize the division of the country inherited from the British administration into fourteen states (and six federal territories) roughly coincident with these languages. These states do not differ as much in size as the American or German states, ranging from 4 to 63 million,[10] with the average of about 25 million. Actually this distribution of languages among states roughly resembles the European pattern, as represented in the Council of Europe (see chapter 21), while the differences between these languages are much greater than are those between the European languages. The range of religious differences is also far wider.[11] In terms of over-all patterning, therefore, a considerably looser federal relationship than the present one of the Indian Union would seem to be indicated in a fully developed bureaucratized and democratized India.

The extent and variety of the linguistic conflicts and problems have by no means decreased as a result of the creation of states based on linguistic communities.[12] "Linguism" has appeared as a form of chauvinism of a prevalent language group. The States Reorganization Commission noted that "already in some of the States a large percentage of members in the Legislature know only one language and this trend is likely to become more and more pronounced. In some states even ministers only know one language."[13] As a result, the states are becoming more and more inclined to oppress the linguistic minorities within their border, and the national government has not been very active or successful in upholding the constitutional provision for the protection of such minorities.[14] Riots and other disturbances have been the result. There were "language riots" in Assam, in Bombay, and in Madras; there were the Punjabi-Suba agitations in the Punjab; there has developed an urgent demand for the recognition of Urdu as a regional language in Uttar Pradesh and Bihar with their Hindi majorities; there have also been border disputes, related to linguistic minorities, such as that between Mysore and Maharashtra. It all seems part of a clear trend toward greater linguistic and cultural autonomy throughout India.

There is little question that some of these tensions are related to the desperate economic plight of India. If it were possible to raise the standard of living rapidly, and if the federal government were the prime promoter of such improvement in the condition of the masses, the language problem would become less serious. As it is, it provides a potent weapon in the hands of demagogues and a source of endless quarrels. The fine hopes that are frequently expressed by scholars are not likely to be realized under such conditions. We are told that "some Indians feel that the least harmful way out of the present difficulty might be an improved education in the regional languages and also in Hindi and English, combined with a general attitude of tolerance and patience."[15] True enough, but the top-heavy federal system of India makes it unlikely, and besides, such trilingualism is not practical for the masses of even a gifted people. In highly literate and democratic Switzerland, the general electorate speaks only one language, though the Swiss are usually familiar with one other (see chapter 20); besides, its languages are closely

related to Indo-Germanic tongues. It would seem that an
alien *lingua franca* like English (corresponding to Latin in
medieval Europe) would have the best chance in India, especially as it provides the much needed link with the outside
world for the governing elite. (English-language dailies have
the largest circulation in India: one million as against half
that for Hindi.) Vigorous development of the several languages, combined with retention of the increasing pluralism
of such an increasingly federal India, might become a source
of strength, as the component states mature into vigorous
democratic societies.

NOTES TO CHAPTER 18

1. See, for example, S. A. H. Haqqi, "Federalism, Single Dominant Party
and the Problem of Linguistic Autonomy in India," a paper read before
IPSA (Geneva Congress, 1964), p. 2; but others are of the opposite opinion, for example, N. Srinivasan, *Democratic Government in India* (1954),
p. 147: "The federal character of the Constitution is indisputable. . . . The
new constitution of India has effected an adjustment of federal-state relations suited to the conditions of India that is *sui generis*. . . . " The latter
position seems sounder in terms of our view of federalism. See also Morris-
Jones, *op. cit.* (note 11, chapter 7).

2. Shri N. V. Gadgil, *Constituent Assembly Debates*, Vol. XI, p. 657 (as
cited by Haqqi). For an admirable review of the extensive literature on
Indian federalism and its background, see T. J. Leonard's essay in Livingston,
op. cit. (note 9, chapter 1), pp. 87 ff.

3. S. V. Kogekar, "Federalism in India," a paper read before the Oxford
Round Table on Federalism (1963), *passim*.

4. *Ibid.*, p. 6.

5. Paul Friedrich, "Language and Politics in India," *Daedalus* (Summer,
1962). Haqqi gives the following figures for the ten major language groups:
Hindi, Urdu, Punjabi, and Hindustani—149,944,311; Telegu—32,999,916;
Marathi—27,049,522; Tamil—26,546,764; Bengali—25,121,674; Gujarati—16,310,-
771; Kannada—14,471,764; Malayalam—13,380,109; Oriya—13,153,909; and
Assamese—4,988,226; he notes that there are besides 47 other Indian and
tribal languages, though not all of them are languages with a literary record.
(For the distribution among the states, see note 10.) Article 351 of the Constitution recognizes 14 languages; in addition to the ones cited, these include Kashmiri, Punjabi, Sanskrit, and Urdu. It will be noted that Punjabi
and Urdu, as well as Hindustani, are lumped together with Hindi in the
above official statistics, obviously in order to swell the size of Hindi to make
it look to be by far the largest group; such lumping is not accepted by
speakers of these languages, of whom there are many millions of each.

6. M. P. Desai, *Our Language Problem* (1956); B. R. Ambedkar, *Thoughts
on Linguistic States* (1955); see also the article cited in note 5. See in addition

S. S. Harrison, *The Most Dangerous Decades—Language Policy in Multilingual States* (1957); W. H. Morris-Jones, *The Government and Politics of India* (1964).

7. Paul Friedrich, *op. cit.,* p. 552.

8. C. Rajagopalachari, *Tamil Culture* (1959), p. 210.

9. See Lloyd and Suzanne Rudolph, *op. cit.* (note 12, chapter 7).

10. As reported by Paul Friedrich, the states are, with population (in terms of millions) and language in parentheses: Andhra (31—Telegu); Assam (5—Assamese); West Bengal (26—Bengali); Bihar (38—Hindi); Madras (29—Tamil); Orissa (14—Oriya); Punjab (16—Punjabi, Hindi); Uttar Pradesh (63—Hindi); Rajastan (15—Rajastan, Hindi); Jamnu and Kashmir (4—Kashmiri, Urdu); Mysore (19—Kannada); Kerala (14—Malayalam); from S. Sarkar, *Hindustani Yearbook* (1959), pp. 402 ff.

11. Harrison drew this comparison when he wrote: "In size and resources, the ten regional components of the Indian Union can properly be compared to the sovereign nations of Europe." In S. S. Harrison, "The Challenge to Indian Nationalism," *Foreign Affairs,* Vol. 34 (1956), p. 620.

12. Haqqi, *op. cit.,* p. 8; see also references in note 6 above.

13. Haqqi, *op. cit.,* p. 11; see also Hugh Tinker, *India and Pakistan* (1962) pp. 134 ff., and the *Report of the Official Language Commission* (New Delhi, 1965), pp. 451 ff. Haqqi here reports the case of a premier of Madras who, coming from below, had so little command of Hindi (and English) that he had to use an interpreter for his conference with the Prime Minister of India!

14. K. V. Rao, *Parliamentary Democracy in India* (1961), chapter VI, Part II, especially pp. 190–95.

15. Paul Friedrich, *op. cit.,* p. 558; see also Haqqi, *op. cit.,* at the end. Rao, *op. cit.,* p. 286, wisely comments that "it is obvious that it is the particular weakness of the Constitution that it will create constant friction between the Center and the States . . . and that this constant friction will weaken the solidarity of the country much more than a real federation with greater provincial autonomy could have done." This is the conclusion of his chapter IX on the Indian federal problem. See also Morris-Jones, *op. cit.* (note 11, chapter 7).

19

ITALY: REGIONALISM AND FEDERALISM

THE VIOLENT AND AGGRESSIVE ACTIVITIES of a South Tyrolese (Austrian) minority against the Italian authorities have highlighted a problem which has been an issue in Italy for many years: regionalism and federalism. It would have seemed natural for Italy to adopt a federal regime, in view of Italian history which, like German history, has been characterized by much intense localism; many of her great cities, like Florence and Venice, formed independent states until modern times. There were strong advocates for such a federal form. But the historic role of the Piedmontese monarchy in the liberation and unification of Italy, the *Risorgimento,* led to the establishment of a unitary state under the house which had acted as liberator. The excesses of Fascist centralism helped to bring on a reaction in the direction of regionalism, which was reinforced by the transformation of Italy into a democratic republic. In the new constitution (of 1948), regionalism was proclaimed and organized as the future form of Italy (Articles 114–133). But only part of it has since become reality.[1]

The constitution calls for the establishment of two types

of regions, the regular ones and the special regions. The latter are granted particular forms of autonomy by means of statutes which are considered constitutional and which are to be adopted for each region in light of its particular needs and requirements. Curiously enough, it is the special regions that have come into being, while the regular ones have not so far been organized, the parliament having failed to adopt the necessary legislation.[2] The constitution itself provides for a system of concurrent powers under which the regions, once established, were to have a carefully circumscribed share in the legislative power, subject to three important limitations. The first of these is of course the requirement of constitutionality. Second, such regional laws must be, the constitution provides, "within the limits of the fundamental principles established by the laws." In other words, they implement national legislation, rather than supplant it; furthermore, such legislation must not be "in conflict with the interests of the nation or other regions." Third, every legislative act passed by the council of the region is subject to objection by the national government,[3] such objections to be communicated by a commissioner who also "supervises the administrative functions" of the national government, and "coordinates" those exercised by the region; the legality of administrative acts is to be subject to a special body which the law is to establish. It is clear that these "limitations" are not very different from those to which states or cantons are subject under a federal regime. The range of functions provided was quite considerable, too: Besides the obvious one of organizing their own offices and administrative agencies, the regional legislative competency was to include communal districting; local police; fairs and markets; public welfare; health and hospitals; professional and handicraft instruction; museums and libraries; city planning; tourist and hotel business; intraregional street car and bus lines; intraregional roads; aqueducts and public works; lake navigation and ports; mineral and thermal springs; stone quarries and bogs; hunting; fishing; agriculture and forests; handicrafts. There was also a permissive clause enabling the extension of this list by constitutional legislation; besides "the power to enact regulations for the implementation of the laws of the Republic may be delegated to the regions." What the afore-cited provisions show is that Italy's regional plan closely approximated the pattern of a "unitary federal state" such as Brazil or India. It was characteristic of such an attempt at federalizing that it provided the structural pattern for the regions: "the regional council, the regional committee and its president" (Article 121). The first was to be the legislative organ, the second, the executive, and the third, the president, was to represent the region, to promulgate regional laws and regulations, and to direct such delegated administration as the national government might wish to have the region administer. It is significant that the further organization of the region was to be embodied in a "statute" which, unlike the state constitutions in federal regimes, was to be subject to approval by the national legislature.[4] It should be remembered, however, that the constitution of an American state, when joining the Union, also is subject to congressional approval, and similar provisions prevail elsewhere.

These provisions apply, generally speaking, to the special regions, which are simply included in the list given in the constitution.[5] Special statutes have, in the case of the five special regions, actually been adopted (Sicily, 1946; Sardinia, Trentino–Alto Adige, and Val d'Aosta, 1948; and Friuli–Venezia Giulia, 1964). The reason undoubtedly is that in these regions there exists a strong sense of local identity, reinforced by more pronounced cultural differentiation, including linguistic minorities—French-speaking in the Val d'Aosta, German-speaking in Trentino–Alto Adige (South Tyrol). These facts are related to other givens: Three of the special regions border on foreign states in which the minority found in the region is the majority, and two are islands. In Sicily a strong separatist movement sprang up toward the end of World War II, which the grant of regional autonomy headed off; but quite apart from that, islands generally are characterized by a strong sense of insular individuality. The special situation of these regions in each instance accounts for the larger autonomy and has worked reasonably well in all but Trentino–Alto Adige.

The special statutes which have been adopted for the five special regions have, in general, followed the pattern laid out in the constitutional provisions summarized above. Regional competence has, however, been more broadly defined. In the case of the Trentino, the arrangements are reinforced by a treaty between Italy and Austria. Even so, the limitations set down by the constitution have been operative; the national government has often objected to regional laws, and where no agreement could be reached, the issues have been settled by the Constitutional Court. The court has been inclined to favor the national government and to restrict regional competence.[6] Two of the regions, Sardinia and Val d'Aosta, have functioned effectively; their regional governments have succeeded in satisfying both the local electorate and the national authorities. The experience in Sicily is very much less satisfactory. Regional politics is fraught with corruption, clientilism, and factionalism (*trasformismo*). Dubious alliances and coalitions of incompatible parties have given the region very inadequate governments, which have failed to concern themselves with many of the tasks assigned to a region, notably education, welfare, and agriculture. In spite of such inadequacies, Sicily has developed rapidly, due to fiscal and financial incentives provided by the region, reinforced and to a considerable extent promoted by public corporations of the Italian state. In any case, Sicily has depended a good deal more upon national support than other regions.[7] Friuli–Venezia Giulia has only recently been organized; it is too early to evaluate the setup. The really serious problems have developed in Trentino–Alto Adige. Here radical elements of the Austrian minority of Tyrolese have carried on a relentless resistance in defense of their local culture and, more especially, their right to use German in school and public life. Feelings run very high and acts of violence have punctuated a rather tortuous effort on the part of both Italian and Austrian authorities to cope with the situation. The Austrian minority tends to feel that it was unfair to create a region in which the Italians have a majority, when actually one of the provinces, namely Bolzano, has a German majority. Regionalism appears to them as an attempt to escape from protecting the minority (and incidentally to violate the letter and spirit of the treaty between Italy and Austria).[8] For the region controls the main functions of local interest, and the demand has crystallized for giving these functions back to the provinces. As a result, the two provinces have been granted greater autonomy than is possessed by other Italian provinces. What this means is that decentralization rather than regionalism has provided the key to the attenuation of a difficult problem of the kind that minorities present. It may, however, be questioned whether a genuine federal order, with Bolzano (South Tyrol) in a special federal relationship to the rest of Italy, would not better serve to resolve the issue than the present half-measures. This might be particularly true if administrative delegation (see chapter 8) were made an integral part of such a scheme. As we saw, the constitution provides that "the state may, by law, delegate to the region the exercise of administrative functions." This provision deserves a few additional comments.

As suggested above, the constitutional provision seems to place the Italian regions in a position similar to that of the Swiss cantons or the German *Länder*. But the difficulty is that the regions do not possess adequate financial resources for handling this sort of delegated administration on their own, so that it has to be supported by the national government. It therefore hardly contributes to local autonomy, but rather the opposite. This could of course be altered by giving the regions adequate tax resources. But Italian students of these matters are skeptical concerning the possibilities. They argue that so much regular administration today in Italy is carried out by special agencies with their own regional divisions that a delegation of administrative execution to the regions from the traditional central administration would complicate the situation, would cause additional financial burdens, and would weaken democracy.[9]

NOTES TO CHAPTER 19

1. Gaspare Ambrosini, *Autonomia Regionale e Federalismo* (probably 1955).

2. Comitato Nazionale per la Celebrazione del primo decennale della Promulgazione della Costituzione, *Raccolta di scritti sulla Costituzione,* (5 vols., 1958).

3. Subject, however, to the provision that the regional Council could reaffirm the law by absolute majority; if, in such a case, the national government did not wish to abide by the regional decision, it could submit the issue to the constitutional court, and has repeatedly done so in the conflicts with the special regions.

4. See Piero Calamandrei and Alessandro Levi, *Commentario sistematico alla Costituzione Italiana* (1950), Vol. II, pp. 225–379 (Giorgio Miele).

5. Article 131 lists the following regions: Piedmont, Val d'Aosta, Lombardy, Trentino—Alto Adige, Veneto, Friuli–Venezia Giulia, Liguria, Emilia–Romagna, Tuscany, Umbria, Marche, Lazio, Abruzzi and Molise, Campania, Puglia, Basilicata, Calabria, Sicilia, Sardinia. Besides noting that the list includes the special regions to which therefore the general provisions presumably apply, one might recall that each of these regions includes two or more of the traditional provinces which are subdivisions of the unitary state.

6. Taylor Cole, "Three Constitutional Courts: A Comparison," *American Political Science Review,* Vol. LIII (1959), pp. 963 ff. Gottfried Dietze, "Judicial Review in Europe," *Michigan Law Review,* Vol. 55 (1957), pp. 539 ff., and "Decline and Emergence of Judicial Review," *Virginia Law Review,* Vol. 44 (1958), pp. 1233 ff. Edward McWhinney, *Constitutionalism in Germany and the Federal Constitutional Court* (1962), especially chapter I.

7. John Clarke Adams and Paolo Barile, *The Government of Republican Italy* (1961), pp. 120–23, discuss the regions. They cite with approval a statement by Luigi Einaudi (former President of Italy) from "Che cosa reimarebbe allo stato?" in *Prediche inutili, despensa sesta* (1959), pp. 335–59, especially p. 357, that Trentino subsidies amounted to less than a third of the subsidies, percentagewise, of those to Sicily; or, as they put it, "if the subsidies going to Trentino–Alto Adige were applied [to all of Italy] the regions

would be receiving 18 to 19 per cent of the state's annual income, while if
the Sicilian subsidies were applied, the regions would be spending 61 to
62 per cent of the annual Italian national income." I believe what is meant
is not the national income, but the national tax revenue. Even so, the
argument does not seem very decisive; similar figures of contrast could be
worked out for the poorest members of other federal systems.

8. It is indicative of the seriousness of the issues that Italy as a member of
the EEC has threatened to block Austria's association with the European
Communities, if the violence continues. It is difficult to see how the Austrian
government can hope to stop violence in a territory it does not control.

9. For the range of problems here discussed, see the contributions to a
symposium held in 1963 at Florence and published under the title *Symposium Internazionale sui problemi della regione e del governo locale* (Milan,
1963), especially the contributions by V. Crisafulli and L. Giovenco; see also P.
Virga, *La Regione* (1949), C. Mortati, "Alcuni aspetti dell'ordinamento
regionale" in *Studi sulla Costituzione*, Vol. III (1958), and A. Predieri,
Pianificazione e Costituzione (1963). I would also like to acknowledge with
thanks the help received on this section from Dr. Stefano Passigli.

20

SWITZERLAND: DIRECT POPULAR ACTION FOR CULTURAL INTEGRATION

AMONG THE MANY INTERESTING ASPECTS of Swiss federalism which are the fruit of a long history reaching back into the middle ages, we have selected the multilingual and multicultural aspects in relation to referenda as perhaps the most relevant to the contemporary situation. It is high-lighted by recent serious difficulties in the canton of Bern over a French-speaking minority in the Jura. In many ways this conflict is particularly revealing, since the Swiss, as so many others in other lands, have prided themselves on the absence of any such disturbances between their cultural components. Switzerland's problem would seem to be aggravated by the fact that all but her tiniest cultural group—the Romansch-speaking minority of 1 per cent in the mountains of Eastern Switzerland—are related to one of the surrounding great powers: the German-, the French-, and the Italian-speaking Swiss each bordering on their cousins' respective land. To be sure, the Swiss have developed a very strong sense of identity and the language they speak is for many of them no ground for feel-

ing related to Germany, France, or Italy, except in a cultural
sense. But since cultural affinities often carry strong political
implications, Switzerland has in the past become emotionally
involved in the conflicts between these powers.[1]

The distribution of the four languages in 1960 (by mother
tongue) gave German 74.4 per cent, French 20.2 per cent,
Italian 4.1 per cent, and Romansch 1.0 per cent. If the recent
immigrants from Italy who have become resident are added,
the Italian percentage rises to 9.5 per cent, with the others
slightly reduced accordingly. In any case, it is clear that the
German-speaking Swiss far outnumber the other three, and
have done so throughout Swiss history. Yet, a tradition of
moderation and fair play has prevented this majority from
over-playing its hand; years ago it was pointed out that, for
example, in appointments to the Swiss civil service, the minorities have been given more than their proportional share
of appointments.[2] The Swiss in other words developed a habit
of equal treatment for all Swiss, regardless of their nationality, which has served to build a powerful civic pride in
Switzerland. The authoritarian aberrations in their three
powerful neighbors have further reinforced this sentiment in
the present century.

Yet in spite of their strong national sentiment, the Swiss
have preserved an equally strong cantonal spirit (*Kantön-
ligeist*), a local patriotism which has caused particularly the
more conservative elements to guard with jealous concern,
sometimes bordering on pettiness, the prerogatives of each
canton, no matter how small. Religious, cultural, and economic interests and beliefs combine to give each canton its
sense of individuality, regardless of whether its citizens belong to one or another of the language groups. To be sure, a
large majority of the cantons are unilingual, but since three
of the four languages are official and all four are "national"
languages, every citizen, even if in a canton with another
language, is fully protected in his rights. The recognition of

Romansch as the fourth national language is of relatively recent date, and had to be adopted by referendum, as do all constitutional amendments. It is characteristic of the Swiss general attitude that 92 per cent of the voters and all of the cantons voted for it.

This brings us squarely up against the use and problem of the referendum as an instrumentality of federal government. In Switzerland and for the Swiss, it incorporates their belief in full-fledged democracy, that is to say, their belief that the people should be the final arbiters on basic questions. Not a supreme court, but the people are the umpire. This is accomplished by two provisions, one that calls for a referendum on all constitutional amendments, the other that a not inconsiderable group of Swiss citizens—at least 30,000—may use the initiative in requesting a referendum on any law (with some exceptions as noted below). They may also, by initiative of 50,000, demand that a constitutional amendment be submitted to the people.[3] These instrumentalities are familiar from American practice, but it is important to add that since these instrumentalities were embodied in the constitution in 1874, they have been extensively used and have, generally speaking, acted as a curb rather than a promoter of change. There can be little question, though, that such methods of direct popular action have been working fairly satisfactorily in Switzerland. As far as the federal relationship is concerned, they serve to emphasize the fact that the people of each canton constitute a separate and distinct entity with a substantial degree of autonomy. Even so, governmentalism (*étatisme*) has steadily progressed, and by such referenda as that on economic questions (1947), the Swiss people have not only by popular, but also by cantonal majority sanctioned the development of a closely regulated market economy.[4] Such an act would seem to prove the viability of the Swiss system. It is noteworthy in this connection that the federal constitution requires that cantonal constitutions be submitted to popular referendum. Besides, the cantons provide for referendum and initiative in many different forms. Here, too, they are very widely practiced and have given acceptable results.[5] An important addition was made in 1921 when it was decided that treaties with foreign powers lasting more than fifteen years must, when requested, be submitted to the people—a logical implication of the basic conviction that all important matters should be settled by the people themselves. Even with so highly literate an electorate as the Swiss, it may be doubted whether this provision is sound. Nonetheless, Swiss experience in the past was well summarized some years ago: "Direct legislation in Switzerland has not realized all the extravagant anticipations of its friends. But on the other hand, it has completely falsified the dismal prophecies of chaos and revolution. . . . It has become a vital and freely functioning part of the Swiss political organism."[6] The recurrent refusal of the general electorate to sanction constitutional and legislative measures designed to benefit particular interest groups suggests that the referendum is an integrating mechanism. It is a mechanism, more particularly, for developing the federal relationship between the Swiss people at large and the people of each and every canton on a basis of mutuality and compromise. This aspect of the matter is central to Swiss federalism with its emphasis on the will of the people. Such an autonomous will is epitomized by the notion of a linguistic autonomy (*Sprachenhoheit*), which gives the cantons the right to fashion their own language policy within the framework of the principles provided by the constitution. It may defend its own language and culture as much as its people deem desirable. This principle was put by a leading Swiss constitutional lawyer as follows: "It is now a tacitly recognized principle that each territory (not necessarily a canton) should be able to retain its traditional language regardless of immigrants of other languages, and consequently that linguistic boundaries should not be shifted."[7] The principle was generally accepted by the Swiss, but not by the recent immigrants from Italy who feel no obligation to assimilate to what they consider an alien environment. As a result, serious tensions and animosities have developed which used to be quite alien to Switzerland. On the whole, though, the linguistic frontiers of Switzerland have remained rather fixed, in spite of considerable mobility of the working force. According to the 1960 census, the unilingual cantons had between 82 and 99 per cent of their citizens belonging to the particular dominant language group, and the bilingual ones were divided into clearly defined areas, where the percentages were similarly high. One might add that of more than 3,000 communes in Switzerland, only six have changed their linguistic regime since 1848.[8] The many local dialects spoken in German Switzerland have helped in maintaining this stability.

There has, however, developed a very sharp conflict in one of the bilingual cantons, namely Bern, in which the capital city is located. That capital city itself presents some difficult problems, especially that of the education of the children of civil servants from the French-speaking cantons.[9] But these we leave aside in order to give brief attention to the issues involved in the position of the French-speaking minority. This minority is concentrated in the northern part of the canton bordering on France, inhabiting the valleys in the mountain range of the Jura. This district was added to the canton in 1815; it is Catholic, which has precipitated difficulties with the Protestant majority and helped in maintaining a sense of local identity. But only since World War II has the conflict become bitter, occasionally even leading to violence. After the war, the *Jurassiens* banded together and formulated demands, including that of separating from Bern and becoming an independent canton. Short of that they asked for various reforms, including educational autonomy and decentralization of the public service. These demands all culminated in the insistence that the French- and German-speaking parts of Bern were two separate and distinct peoples. The cantonal authorities met some of these demands, including the constitutional recognition of a separate and distinct *peuple Jurassien* and equality of the two languages. But the concessions proved inadequate, and the clamor for a separate canton became more insistent. In 1960, the population of the Jura district amounted to 131,000 (compared to the 759,000 in the rest of the canton), but that figure is well above the population of several other cantons. Consequently there is widespread sympathy in other parts of Switzerland for the *Jurassien* claim. Some experts believe that a nation-wide referendum would favor the *Jurassiens*. However, there are dissensions within the group itself, and when the canton held a referendum in 1959 on the issue, not only did the Bernese at large reject the proposal, but it did not even receive a majority in the territory itself. Four out of eleven districts in the Jura territory, for economic and religious reasons, refused to go along with the demand for a separation. The issue has not come to rest. On the contrary, there has been an intensification of separatist feeling. Many Swiss feel that the attitude of the *Jurassien* is rather un-Swiss and contrary to their tradition. The violent nationalist sentiment is certainly unlike the feeling of most Swiss, although there have been rumblings in the Ticino (Italian) and in the Grisons (Romansch). At the same time, it is noteworthy that all of the agitation has rarely, if ever, been anti-Swiss. Rather, it has always remained within the bounds of loyalty toward Switzerland as a whole. It may well prove necessary to fall back upon this loyalty and to settle the issue through national referendum.

In conclusion, one can say that the Swiss have succeeded in handling nationality difficulties successfully by means of a number of democratic instrumentalities, more especially direct popular action through initiative and referendum. The referendum is useful in making possible an affirmation of a collective sense of belonging on the part of distinctive constituency, but the problem of how to define that constituency in particular circumstances belongs among the most delicate problems of political strategy.

NOTES TO CHAPTER 20

1. Robert C. Brooks, *Civic Training in Switzerland* (1930), still seems to me the most balanced general treatment of the problems here involved. A recent study of the multilingual problems by Kenneth D. McRae, *Switzerland—Example of Cultural Coexistence* (1964), brings this special phase up to date in a very concise fashion.

2. Carl J. Friedrich and Taylor Cole, *Responsible Bureaucracy—A Study of the Swiss Civil Service* (1934). Article 107 of the Swiss Constitution requires that the Federal Tribunal (Supreme Judicial Court) should include representatives of all the official language groups.

3. Brooks, *op. cit.*, pp. 107 ff. See also Friedrich and Cole, *op. cit.* (note 2 above), especially pp. 55 ff. The most searching study of the Swiss practice of referendum and initiative is a Swedish one by A. Brusewitz, *Folkromröstningsinstitutet i den Schweizeska Demokratien* (1923).

4. W. E. Rappard, *La Constitution Fédérale de la Suisse—1848–1948* (1948), pp. 328 ff.

5. F. Fleiner, *Schweizerisches Bundesstaatsrecht* (1932), pp. 56–58.

6. Brooks, *op. cit.*, p. 11.

7. Walther Burckhardt, *Kommentar* (3d ed., 1931), p. 806.

8. McRae, *op. cit.*, p. 13, citing *Res Publica*, Vol. IV (Brussels, 1962), p. 254. This issue of *Res Publica*, entitled "La question linguistique en Suisse," contains other valuable contributions, especially by Dr. H. Weilenmann, the author of the most comprehensive study on the Swiss language situation, *Die Vielsprachige Schweiz: Eine Lösung des Nationalitätenproblems* (1925). Although now in some respects dated, it is still a basic source.

9. McRae, *op. cit.*, pp. 57 ff.

21

UNITED EUROPE: AN EMERGENT FEDERAL ORDER?

UNITED EUROPE, or, more specifically, Europe in the process of federalizing the relations among its members, presents some very special issues to the student of federal and regional relations. One of the industrially advanced regions of the world, except for some retarded entities, like Sicily and Ireland, it represents the greatest conglomeration of people within a small territory. Its population of more or less 200 million (the exact figure depending upon what is included) is living on a territory not much larger than Texas. Formerly the "hub of the Universe," it is now being united not only by its defense needs, but by the economic problems which the disintegration of its several colonial empires has created. At its core, France, Germany, Italy, and the Benelux countries have formed the Community of the Six, the primary focus of which is the European Economic Community (the Common Market), a treaty-based confederation for the purpose of developing a united economic policy. Many more states are loosely associated in the Council of Europe, which preceded the EEC, having come into being in 1950. In addition to the Six,

Great Britain, the Scandinavian countries, and a number of other smaller states participate in this international union. It has primarily promoted some general patterns of cooperation through conventions in the social and cultural field, including the setting up of an arbitration procedure for alleged violations of an agreed-on bill of human rights;[1] unfortunately some important powers have been slow in ratifying this convention. These two organizations of a federalizing Europe are implemented by a special union in the military field, the Western European Union (WEU), brought into being in the sequel of the failure to agree on a European Defense Community; the WEU has not played a very vital role, since its functions overlap with those of NATO. Significant mostly as a forum and a means for promoting all-European economic cooperation is the Organization for Economic Cooperation and Development (OECD), formerly the Organization for European Economic Cooperation (OEEC), which renders valuable service also in the field of banking and currency.[2]

As a result of these and other specific functional ties, it is extremely difficult to define the European federal relationship at the present time. Special issues, such as that of supra-nationality—meaning the question of whether any of these functional bodies have an authority transcending the authority of the national governments which cooperate in them—are rather artificial in view of the fact that the formal juristic situation is continually being superseded by custom and usage shaping specific developments in particular fields. But there can be little question that the lack of a unifying and integrating *political* organization is causing very serious difficulties. Numerous proposals for creating such an organization have been put forward in recent years. Men of great experience, such as former EEC President Hallstein, have often stated it as their conviction that economic cooperation cannot hope to succeed without adequate political organization to back it. But none of the plans and proposals have so far succeeded, or even come near doing so. The most advanced of these proposals, the draft of a constitution for a European Political Community, fashioned by an *Ad Hoc* Assembly in the winter of 1952–53, may be considered a high-water mark which Europe is now farther than ever from reaching again. Yet, even this "advanced" mechanism was far from adequate as a framework of European political unity, and it was only meant to apply to the Community of the Six.[3]

If the question is asked, why the federalizing process has been so slow and has recently been retrogressive, the answer is not simple. Personal factors, such as President de Gaulle's hostility toward any kind of supranational authority, undoubtedly have played a considerable role and continue to do so. But they could not have done so if support for a federal union in Europe were stronger in the respective constituencies; a France truly committed to European unity would withdraw its support from a leader who refused to participate effectively in this task.[4] The more powerful factors feeding European disunity are both economic and political, while the cultural field has experienced a much greater readiness to shape a European future. Among the political factors, the varying intensity of apprehension concerning the aggressive designs of the Soviet Union is quite important. Such fears have varied not only between periods; they have also been much more intense in Germany than in Britain, more intense among farmers than workers, and so forth. Under these circumstances it can hardly be considered surprising that initiatives promoted at one time and by one power falter at a succeeding period of thaw or *Entspannung*. It is more than doubtful that this situation will change noticeably in the years to come.

Even so, as pointed out earlier (see chapter 11), the EEC continues to attract states seeking both membership and association, and Switzerland has joined the Council of Europe, after many years of hesitation.[5] There can be little doubt that the European Community is growing; numerous informal bonds are being created through the multiplication of human contacts in business, in cultural relations, and so on. There are today developing in Europe intimate working relations between parties, research institutes, publications, and other communication media that were rare in the interwar years. At the grassroots level, communes are developing special links, the so-called *jumelages,* through which French, Italian, German, Belgian, and Dutch—and indeed British— local governments cooperate in promoting a European sense of community and a belief in the potentialities of solving common problems jointly.[6] From all these different sources, in themselves small, spring activities which presuppose an eventually united Europe with a common citizenship and common foreign and defense policy. Indeed, certain nationality problems which have plagued European states, such as the Belgian and Italian ones we have analyzed, will become attenuated and may eventually be reduced to the kind of internal quarrel which the question of the *Jura* amounts to within Switzerland.

The most significant lesson which the student of federalism can derive from the long drawn-out federalizing process of European unification is that even very loose bonds may have high significance, and that it is not necessary to insist upon the outworn issues of sovereignty when handling the highly pragmatic issues of a federal relationship, nor to try to give such a relationship a permanent, let alone an irrevocable form. It is possible to let such a relationship evolve, and to solve specific problems as they emerge.

At the same time, European experience also suggests the inherent dangers of a loose international federal relationship. Sovereignty may be defined (as it is in Article V of the Swiss constitution) by whatever is left after the supranational competencies have been enumerated; in that case it is a harmless, if somewhat nebulous concept. But if sovereignty is allowed to intrude itself into the federal relationship in its old absolutist sense of an unlimited competence to determine its own range of competencies, as is De Gaulle's inclination, then it becomes destructive of the federal relationship. At bottom, however, the sovereignty issue is merely a symbolic manifestation of a weak federal spirit (see chapter 23).

On the whole, the process of federalizing the Community of the Six has gone forward with sufficient vigor to overcome recurrent setbacks. The desire of Great Britain to join the Community now presents it with its greatest challenge. The fear of General de Gaulle that the inclusion of so different a country as Great Britain would disrupt the difficult process of integration, while arguable, is not shared by the partners of France in the Community. They, on the contrary, incline to believe that a genuinely committed, communitarian Britain would reinforce the federalizing process and help to overcome some of the present reluctance. It is difficult to be sure about such judgments on contingent issues. In some ways the problem resembles that overcome in the federal unification of Germany nearly a hundred years ago; then, the German states were, for reasons somewhat reminiscent of those presented against Britain today by France, urged by Prussia to reject the Hapsburg Empire. It has remained controversial to this day whether the fact that Bismarck's unification policy prevailed was on the whole "right" or not— whatever that may mean. In the case of Europe, any process of uniting the peoples that constitute her "culture," without including such crucial members as Great Britain and the Scandinavians, and indeed Spain, would seem incomplete and not in accordance with world trends.[7]

NOTES TO CHAPTER 21

1. The general literature on the unification movement in Europe has become very voluminous. A good general review of the politics up to the mid-1950's is provided by Ernst B. Haas, *op. cit.* (note 4, chapter 5); for a more

recent assessment, see Arnold J. Zurcher, *The European Community—An Approach to Federal Integration* (1964), pp. 67–115, and, for the preceding period, his *The Struggle To Unite Europe, 1940–1958* (1958). The British view (favorable) is well stated in Uwe W. Kitzinger, *The Politics and Economics of European Integration* (1963). Besides these, the *General Reports on the Activities of the Community,* published by the EEC Commission (Brussels), are an important source, as is the *European Yearbook,* published since 1954 under the auspices of the Council of Europe (The Hague). R. R. Bowie and the author's *Studies in Federalism,* prepared by a group of researchers for the *Ad Hoc* Assembly in 1953, contains an introduction by the author reviewing the background of the draft constitution and its shortcomings.

2. The Commission at Brussels has published a list of all the organizations concerned in the unification movement of Europe.

3. Bowie and Friedrich, *op. cit.* (note 1 above). In the appendix, there is found the text of the draft treaty for a constitution, preceded by the *Resolutions* of the preparatory Study Committee; these latter are more radical.

4. Such an effect can be discerned in the reaction of French farm groups to the "crisis" in the Community precipitated on June 30, 1965 by the French decision not to participate in some of the work. The protests of these groups took strong forms and presumably affected the outcome of the first round of the presidential election in France that fall. Hélène Delorme and Yves Tavernier, *Les Paysans Français et l'Unité Européenne* (forthcoming), have been able to demonstrate this complex phenomenon in detail.

5. May 6, 1963; see *European Yearbook* (1964).

6. This process forms the topic of one of the studies on the political implications of informal community formation, Dr. Rolf Grauhan, *Politische Dimensionen der Europäischen Gemeinschaftsbildung,* ed. Carl J. Friedrich (1968). See also the contributions of Dusan Sidjanski to the above volume and to "The Politics of European Integration" in *Government and Opposition* (1967), Vol. II, pp. 397 ff., and by J. R. Rabier, *ibid.,* pp. 443 ff. See also Karl Deutsch, *op. cit.* (note 2, chapter 6) and the critical comment by Ronald Englehart, *ibid.*

7. See my paper in *Philosophy, Religion, and the Coming World Civilisation—Essays in Honor of William Ernest Hocking* (1966), pp. 330 ff. (This paper also available in German and in French.)

22

YUGOSLAVIA: FAÇADE FEDERALISM?

THE CASE OF YUGOSLAVIA is interesting in connection with trends in contemporary federal relations, because Yugoslavia is a socialist country, which calls itself a popular democracy though outsiders see it as a totalitarian dictatorship. Moreover, it is multilingual and composed of several nationalities, notably the Serbs, the Croats, the Slovenes, the Montenegrins, and the Macedonians. One of its leading constitutional authorities has characterized the position of Yugoslav federalism in light of the 1963 constitutional revision as follows:

> The Yugoslav Federation was formed during the Liberation War and the Socialist Revolution on the basis of the right of every people to self-determination, including the right to form separate states or unite in a federal community. It came into being as a voluntary community of equal and sovereign Yugoslav peoples which constituted a common federal state and simultaneously ensured their individuality in their republics as forms of state organizations.[1]

Such federalism was an important ingredient of Josip Broz's (Tito's) plan, since the preceding regime, before being con-

quered by Hitler's and Mussolini's armies, had been a unitary
state, based upon the hegemony of the Serbs. This hegemony
had been unpopular with the country's other nationality
groups. More especially, the rivalry of Serbs and Croats had
been so violent that the Nazis and Fascists found it to their
advantage to encourage the Croats to set up an independent
state, under the leadership of one Pavelić, who had for many
years been the head of a movement known as the Utascha
(meaning the rebel); members of this movement had mur-
dered the King of Serbia and the French foreign minister in
1934. This "Independent State of Croatia" perished, of course,
with its Fascist protagonists, but it left a heritage of passionate
nationality sentiment, which only a federal order could hope
to assuage to some extent.[2] Such federalism was proclaimed
by Tito, the Communist leader of the popular liberation
army, and himself a Croat, as early as 1943; it was quite in
keeping with the Soviet constitution. The federal system,
while Communist, was to be based upon the equality of the
several nationalities. The constitution of 1946 made this principle the basis of the political order and it has been retained
in its most recent draft.[3] In the "Basic Principles" preceding
the constitution, the principle of self-determination is acknowledged and, just as in the Soviet Union, the right to
secession is explicitly recognized; both are transcended by the
integrating power of the Communist Party, which speaks of
itself as a "union" of Communist parties, but is in fact a
closely integrated monolith under Tito's dictatorial leadership. This fact also finds expression in the constitution itself.
It would lead too far afield to recite here in detail what is
the jurisdiction of the "federation"; it includes virtually all the
economic policy fields which in a socialist country are the
core of government.[4] One of the authors of this constitution,
a jurist of renown, has described the situation as follows: "The
common functions of the working people of Yugoslavia are
made secure by the establishment of a unique social, economic

and political system . . . the federation is responsible for the
establishment, the consolidation, the protection and the development of the socio-economic foundations of socialism."[5]
It is obvious that the federal relationship under such conditions and in light of such goals is bound to be very different
from that prevailing elsewhere. It is more nearly like a cen-
trally directed setup which is built upon a substantial amount
of decentralization. It has been argued that the stress on centralization in the 1946 constitution was even greater than in
the constitution of the Soviet Union of 1936, but this seems
incorrect. The revision of 1963 makes a considerable effort to
protect the member republics (as it does the citizen) by the
establishment of a constitutional court (Articles 231–9). Article 236 provides that "if the constitutional court finds that
the federal law in question does not conform to the constitution of Yugoslavia, it shall decide that, pending termination
of the proceedings, the provisions of the federal law that do
not conform to the constitution shall be inoperative."

Even in the earlier constitution, the requirement for federalizing the exercise of the legislative powers was given at
least formal recognition by the establishment of a "Nationalities' Council," composed of thirty representatives for each
republic and, for the "autonomous" provinces and districts, a
smaller number, namely twenty and fifteen respectively. While
democratic centralism reigned supreme, these provisions had
no more significance than in the Soviet Union. But after
Tito's break with the Cominform in 1948, an explicit rejec-
tion of this centralism, now dubbed "bureaucratic," led to a
search for new approaches. Forms of communal property
were proclaimed the harbingers of genuine socialism as contrasted with the "state capitalism" of Moscow. This did by no
means imply a return to Western democracy; far from it.
Yugoslav Communist theoreticians, notably Eduard Kardelj,
began to stress "socialist democracy" which would be based
upon the direct participation of the producer. The recent

constitution has made these notions more explicit.[6] "The foundation of the socio-economic organization of Yugoslavia comprises free associated labor with the means of production and other socially-owned means of labor, and self-government of the working people in production and distribution of the social product in the working organization and the community."[7] The student of the history of socialist doctrines will readily recognize a turn toward pre-Marxist and syndicalist notions. As a key interpreter comments: "Under the Constitution, the commune is the basic social-political community."[8] The stress on local communities as autonomous entities with their own revenue base is part of a legally decentralized system. The Yugoslav Communists are quite ready to recognize the differences in economic development and to rely upon the communes to cope with the resulting tensions and maladjustments.

It is obvious that such stress upon local groupings involves a substantial degree of decentralization of power. In an intermediate constitution (1953) the federal relationship (equality of nationalities) had been strengthened by transforming the Nationalities' Council into a National Council—a kind of superior rule-making body which was to consider constitutional amendments and basic planning objectives and which could propose laws altering the relations between the federation and the member republics. We know too little about the functioning of this body, and about its relations to the Federal Council (the regular legislature) to form a judgment of its suitability as a "mechanism" for vitalizing the federal relationship. In light of the fact that it has disappeared in the 1963 constitution, it may be presumed that it proved cumbersome, if not unworkable. Space does not permit going into the detailed provisions of the constitution of 1963, including the electoral arrangements. Suffice it to note that the representation of the nationalities is now relegated to one of five "chambers": the Federal Chamber, the Chamber of the Economy, the Chamber of Education and Culture, the Chamber of Social Welfare and Health, and the Politico-Administrative Chamber. Members of the Federal Chamber include the members of the Chamber of Nationalities, which meets for certain purposes, especially constitutional amendments and matters pertaining to the "equality of the peoples and republics." These particular members of the Federal Chamber are elected by the six republics and by the two autonomous units, ten and five respectively. The Federal Chamber is the key body of the Assembly—one author calls it *"the* representative institution of Yugoslavia." It is elected by direct vote, whereas the other chambers are elected by the communal assemblies, except for those of its members who are elected by the republics and the autonomous units. This, it will be remembered, is the Soviet or Council principle which facilitates control by a single party. It seems that the arrangements resemble a situation such as might have existed if the U.S. Senate, when it was indirectly elected, had been a part of the House of Representatives except on those occasions when matters of special concern to the states were to be discussed, which would occasion a special sitting of the Senate. One wonders how such an arrangement might work, but no specific information is available. According to one opinion, "the new constitution preserved the old forms of the protection of the autonomy of the peoples of Yugoslavia,"[9] and that therefore the setting up of these chambers does not modify the bicameral principle. It would seem on the evidence of the constitutional provisions that it certainly modifies, if it does not abolish this principle. If one interprets the Federal Chamber as a "permanent second chamber," it would still seem that it has an integrating rather than a balancing function. Its committees presumably control the execution of the law, and the Federal Executive Council, though responsible to the Assembly at large (which comprises, be it recalled, all five chambers), will more particularly be looking to the Assembly's core chamber—the Federal Chamber—for guidance and supervision.[10] Above them all presides the assembly-elected President who, certainly as long as it is Tito, remains the decisive coordinator of all this activity. It is furthermore explicitly provided that the composition of the Federal Executive Council should also have due regard to the equal representation of the nationalities. Since it seems that various high officials also are members of this Council, it must be a fairly large and rather unwieldy body.

But the most significant innovation of the constitution of 1963 is the introduction of "judicial review," that is to say, the notion that a federal constitutional system needs a judicial umpire to resolve conflicts of jurisdiction and invasions of rights and freedoms. It appears that Yugoslavia has, in this matter, followed the precedent of the Federal Republic of Germany[11] in identifying a specific constitutional jurisdiction. The federal constitutional court is paralleled by constitutional courts in the several republics. This change seems to be in line with a general trend in Communist countries to institute a greater degree of rule of law as a necessary ingredient of an advanced economy and an industrial society. As I put it in discussing this trend, "a secret police may still be needed, because the rigid limitations upon public criticism of the official exercise of power oblige such a regime to search out potential enemies . . . yet no autocratic regime . . . would endure long without providing a measure of believed-in justice."[12] The gradual formation of a substantial amount of consensus has facilitated this development. The development of socialist federalism is an important part of this evolution. Dependent as federalism is upon rules of law, it can only hope to function when a substantial consensus comprising all the citizens provides a countervailing power to the centrifugal propensities of national cultural minorities. Even if it merely achieves the unitary federal state, it is preferable to the centralized monolith of the extremes of totalitarianism.

The stage now reached in the evolution of Yugoslav federalism may be one of "real" as contrasted with façade federalism. The decision of the Yugoslav constitutional commission to try out judicial review, which constitutes a certain break with past practice, may prove to have been the turning point, taking the system beyond the former "socialist legality." It appears to involve an acceptance of the contribution that a measure of constitutionalism and a reasonably "independent" judiciary can make to the functioning of a multinational, federal Communist society.[13]

A great deal depends upon the degree of self-restraint which the Communist Party will exercise in the deployment of its concentrated power. In the Soviet Union, there is little evidence of such self-restraint; the federal order has therefore, in spite of certain operational aspects, largely remained a facade for a centralized political order.[14] But the Soviet Bloc, by contrast, has developed distinct federalistic traits and there are signs which point in the direction of further federalizing of the Bloc, such as the recent policy of Rumania.[15]

NOTES TO CHAPTER 22

1. See Jovan Djordjevic, "Some aspects of federalism in a multinational socialist society," a paper read before the Oxford Round Table of IPSA (1964). See also E. Kardelj, "On the Principles of the Preliminary Draft of the New Constitution," in *The New Yugoslav Law*, Vol. XIII (1962), p. 29.

2. Ladislaus Hory and Martin Broszat, *Der Kroatische Utascha-Staat, 1941–1945* (1964).

3. Article 1 of the Constitution of 1963: "The Federal Socialist Republic of Yugoslavia is a federal state of equal peoples voluntarily united, and a socialist democratic community based on self-government and on the power of the working people."

4. The list is a long one; see Articles 160–162, but especially Article 161.

5. Jovan Djordjevic, "Les Caractéristiques fondamentales de la nouvelle Constitution yougoslave," in *Revue International de Droit Comparé* (1963), pp. 698–99.

6. Articles 6–34, *loc. cit.*

7. Kardelj, *op. cit.* (note 1 above), pp. 19–20.

8. *Ibid.*

9. Djordjevic, *op. cit.* (note 5 above), p. 700; the next quotation *ibid.*

10. Articles 241–251.

11. Edward McWhinney, *Comparative Federalism: States' Rights and*

National Power (1962), chapter 3, and his more detailed *Constitutionalism in Germany and the Federal Constitutional Court* (1962).

12. Carl J. Friedrich and Zbigniew Brzezinski, *Totalitarian Dictatorship and Autocracy*, (2d ed., 1965), chapter 10. See also Alex N. Dragnich, "Recent Political Developments in Yugoslavia," in *Soviet Satellite Nations*, ed. John H. Hallowell (1958), a reprint from *The Journal of Politics* (1958).

13. McWhinney, *op. cit.* (note 6, chapter 3), pp. 80 ff.

14. Klaus von Beyme, "Federal Theory and Party Reality in the Soviet Union" in *Public Policy*, Vol. XIII (1964), pp. 396 ff.

15. Zbigniew Brzezinski, *The Soviet Bloc—Unity and Conflict* (1960; rev. ed. 1967), especially chapters 15 and 16.

PART III

Theoretical Trends

23

APPROACHES AND
CONCLUSIONS

THE REVIEW OF SELECTED ISSUES in contemporary federal relations has, it would seem, shown that federalism is more fully
understood if it is seen as a process, an evolving pattern of
changing relationships rather than a static design regulated
by firm and unalterable rules.[1] This finding ought not to be
misunderstood as meaning that the rules are insignificant;
far from it. What it does mean is that any federal relationship
requires effective and built-in arrangements through which
these rules can be recurrently changed upon the initiative
and with the consent of the federated entities. In a sense, what
this means is that the development (historical) dimension of
federal relationships has become a primary focal point, as contrasted with the distribution and fixation of jurisdictions (the
legal aspect). In keeping with recent trends in political science, the main question is: What function does a federal relationship have?—rather than: What structure?

Obviously, recent trends and issues are related to the dominant themes of contemporary political controversy: nationalism, socialism, planning, the relation to parties and interest

groups (the social structure), the role of opposition, delegated administration, policy and decision-making, international federalism and federal "association." The brief country studies or cases high-lighting other issues and trends provide a body of data which cannot be said to "prove" either the success or the failure, either the desirability or the undesirability of federalism. As in so many other political arrangements, "it all depends." At the same time, there are some fairly clear indications that federalism, like other political instrumentalities and orders, can be more or less adequate, more or less suited to the communal situation and structure which it is intended to serve. The suitability of its patterning depends on the degree of differentiation in the community, the urgency of the common task, the strength of the interests and beliefs in their particular mix of time and place.

Before we consider some of the theoretical responses to this changing situation, a word might be in order about the omission of the United States, the U.S.S.R., Austria, Nigeria, and other federal systems, whether mature or emergent, from the country studies. There is no *one* answer to this question. Obviously, a selection had to be made from among the large number of federal systems now operating or emerging. The reason the United States was omitted is that most readers will be familiar with the ongoing discussion and development in our country, so that references in Part I seemed sufficient and no elaboration through a separate country study seemed required. The Union of Soviet Socialist Republics is so unfamiliar, the operation of its federalism so little known, even to Soviet scholars,[2] that it seemed best to focus attention upon the more open and more fully developed socialist federalism of Yugoslavia. In Austria, the actual working of the federal system as contrasted with the legal norms governing it has only recently been studied.[3] Finally, in Nigeria[4] and some of the other new states, the basis of constitutional traditions is so tenuous that concrete experience, even where known, is not particularly convincing.

In fact, Nigeria, along with the Caribbean Federation,[5] provide interesting cases for the hypothesis that federalism does not work when it is imposed, or at any rate urged, upon dependent territories by departing colonial administrators; that is, it is not a solution to built-in divergencies and basic disunity. The failure of each of these federal schemes can be traced to the same source. And the reason is not far to seek. Unless there exists what we have earlier in our analysis called the "federal spirit," that is to say, a firm determination to maintain both diversity and unity by way of a continuous process of mutual adaptation, a federal order cannot last. If the spirit of unity is very strong, a federal regime is apt to turn into a unitary state; if the centrifugal forces of localism are very powerful, a federal regime is likely to break up into its component parts. Both processes have occurred in the course of the history of federalism.

The federal spirit is manifest in two other somewhat intangible but rather important features of a working federal order: federal loyalty and federal comity.[6] They are not always clearly distinguished, because they tend to overlap. Federal loyalty (*Loyauté fédérale*, or *Bundestreue*) is asked of the component units and their representatives; it expects of them a basic commitment to the over-all needs of the federal system. The extremes of its breakdown are manifested in secession and civil war. But there can be quite a few stages before these extremes are reached. There is, for example, administrative sabotage, at present so common in the southern states of the United States where Negro rights are involved. It is to some extent found in all federal regimes, as indeed in all administrative organizations. There is also nullification of federal legislation, either by connivance at disobedience or outright counterlegislation of the local bodies.

Federal comity, on the other hand, is manifest in the practice of fair play by both federal and local officials. It presupposes a willingness to give the other side a "break," to be ready for compromise wherever serious strains develop, to be, in other words, pragmatic in the approach to problems on which the federal and local authorities are divided or on which their intrinsic interests clash. One of the main arguments for such bodies as the German Federal Council and the Council of Permanent Representatives in the European Communities is that such groups are likely to develop the kind of face-to-face human relationships which make for comity. Comity is oil on the complex machinery of federal regimes. All three, the federal spirit, loyalty, and comity are vital behavioral features of federalism. Without them federal systems become unworkable. We need much more detailed studies on their genesis, their operation, and their possible decline and disintegration.[7] There is then such a thing as "federal behavior." It is a highly pragmatic kind of political conduct as we noted which avoids all insistence upon "agreement on fundamentals" and related forms of politically doctrinaire rigidity.

The rapid expansion of federal regimes and proposals has led to a steady broadening of the theoretical scope of federalism. Nearly thirty years ago one could write that "from an empirical standpoint, an effectively centralized government, a federation, a confederation or league of governments (states), an alliance, an alignment, a 'system' of independent governments (states) and finally completely unrelated governments —all these could be represented as differences of degrees in the relation of governments to the persons subject to their rule."[8] This was the beginning of the end of the traditional juristic notions, preoccupied with problems of sovereignty, of the distribution of competencies, and of the structure of the institutions. As for the latter, the emerging pragmatic and behavioral view recognized that a federal system (or state) could be characterized simply by the fact that its structure "resembles a league in one or more of its organizational features."[9] Federal theory has come a long way since then, and the decisive turn is the recognition of its dynamic aspect: that

federalism implies a *process* of federalizing, as well as a pattern or structure.[10] It is the core of such a theory that a federation is a union of groups, united by one or more common
objectives, rooted in common values, interests, or beliefs, but
retaining their distinctive group character for other purposes.
It unites without destroying the selves that are uniting and is
intended to strengthen them; it constitutes organized cooperation of groups as groups. The nature of the particular
groups which federate will have a decisive impact upon the
particular system. Understood as *implying the process of federalizing,* an emergent federal order may be operating in the
direction of both integration and differentiation; federalizing
being *either* the process by which a number of separate political units, be they states or other associations (churches, trade
unions, parties, and so forth), enter into and develop arrangements for working out solutions together, that is to say, making joint decisions and adopting joint policies on common
problems, *or* the reverse process through which a hitherto
unitary political community, as it becomes differentiated into
a number of separate and distinct political subcommunities,
achieves a new order in which the differentiated communities
become capable of working out separately and on their own
decisions and policies on problems they no longer have in
common.[11] Federalism refers to this process, as it does to the
structures and patterns which the process creates; it also encompasses the belief (ideas and ideologies) which it presupposes and generates. Federal behavior and federalist belief are
part and parcel of federalism.[12]

The extension of the range of vision that federalism in
theory and practice has called for means, as we have shown,
the inclusion of international federalism; that is to say, the
recognition that there is a continuum linking the federal state
with loose leagues on one side, with decentralized systems of
government on the other. It has also meant that the practice
of nongovernmental federated entities is being investigated

and compared with the realities of federal government.[13] These realities themselves have been systematized in the work of a number of writers, notably K. C. Wheare and Edward McWhinney, as well as in the collective work edited by R. R. Bowie and C. J. Friedrich.[14] Wheare was much concerned with developing a "test" of what a federal government is, and he answered that when a system of government embodies "predominantly a division of powers between general and regional authorities, each of which, in its own sphere, is coordinate with the others and independent" then that government is federal.[15] Perhaps the term "autonomous" would more correctly describe the situation than "independent" (since, as in Puerto Rico, independent has come to mean separate and apart), but it is evident that his position is sufficiently flexible to fit the dynamic process of federalizing. Wheare also prepared the ground by asking the functional question: "When is federal government appropriate?" His answer stressed the "desire" of a population to be both united and separate. More recent theory has been inclined to go behind this desire and to stress the community structure underlying federal orders. Wheare related such desire to a variety of factors which have often been recognized and which we have encountered in the preceding analysis again and again: Cultural and linguistic diversity, different social and economic structure and stage of development, religious conflicts, and so forth, have made for the desire to preserve a measure of autonomy, while foreign policy and defense needs, economic development, and related matters have produced the desire for unity. On the basis of a broad-gauged review of how federal government works, the learned author then inquired how adaptable federal governments have proved to be, how flexible they have been in evolving in response to the community's needs. He found them on the whole pretty satisfactory; both in war and in economic crisis federal regimes have displayed a capacity to meet emergency situations, and Wheare concluded that "flexibility and adaptability" can best be achieved through increasing cooperation. He finally arrived at a positive evaluation: it is worthwhile to preserve federal government because federalism provides the means for accomplishing what only ever larger units can hope to do, while at the same time preserving as much diversity as possible.[16]

This is the basic justification for federalism in much other federal theory. Thus, Guy Héraud, in his eloquent plea for a "Europe of nationalities" (*Europe des ethnies*) would have a federalized Europe organize itself into ethnically homogeneous regions, regardless of present state boundaries, whenever such nationalities desire it.[17] Only thus, he thinks, can the "massification" of a United Europe be avoided. "The federation of nationalities is the rational crowning achievement of the liberation of nationalities; it reduces alienation and it establishes peace."[18] He would have nationalities in France, Spain, Italy, and other countries, the Bretons, the Alsatians, the Basques, the Catalans, the Tyrolese, and others like them form themselves, if they wished, into autonomous regions; it is in such a context that problems like the Belgian one may be attenuated, if not resolved. Profoundly impressed with the sacrifices imposed upon national minorities by the modern national state, Héraud sees federalism as the one and only remedy for such self-alienation.[19]

It is in keeping with this analysis, specifically addressed to the problems of an emergent Europe, that McWhinney suggests that the formal contests in existing federal systems "mask" contests "between differing ethnic-cultural communities."[20] Such a view is natural enough in the case of a Canadian scholar; he rightly compares it to the racial conflict in the United States. We have seen in our case studies that it is a recurrent problem. It high-lights a basic distinction, he believes, between pluralistic and monistic federalism—a dichotomy which it would seem more realistic to describe in terms of more or less federalism, of looser or closer federalism. He himself points the way by emphasizing the importance of federal "comity," which we just discussed.

All this experience appears in a different light, if the analyst happens to be disillusioned about the working of federalism. Such a view has been presented by William H. Riker, but without producing any significant new theoretical insight. Apart from some unfamiliar terms for familiar facts, the critical evaluation culminates in so extravagant a statement as that "if in the United States one approves of Southern white racists, then one should approve of American federalism," the reason being that "in pure theory . . . what one ought to seek to abrogate for federalism is a system of minority decision that imposes high external costs on everybody other than the minority."[21] In so far as this means a high degree of flexibility, we have seen that earlier theorists have been well aware of this need; more recently, the understanding of federalism as process has made the point paramount. Thus, the criticism is overstated; nonetheless it is well worth stressing that federalism, like all political arrangements, has its weak as well as its strong side.

The cost of federalism has lately seemed particularly high in the field of civil rights. The question has been becoming more insistent as to whether traditional, judicial methods of enforcing those rights which federal law guarantees are going to be adequate to the task. It has rightly been pointed out that the approach in the past has been in terms of the personal rights of the individual; by contrast, the rights of Negroes are those of large groups of people. As a key federal official involved in this situation has put it: "Those who say that civil rights issues cut into the fabric of federalism, are correct." He added: "The loss of faith in law—the usefulness of federal law and the fairness of local law—is gaining very rapidly among Negro and white civil rights workers."[22] He cited with approval the dissent of Justice John Marshall Harlan in 1883. In questioning the majority's view that Congress could not

"independently of the action or non-action of the States" legislate to protect federally guaranteed rights, Harlan argued
that "not only the foundations upon which the national su-
premacy has always securely rested will be materially disturbed, but we shall enter upon an era of constitutional law,
when the rights and freedom and American citizenship cannot receive from the nation that efficient protection which
heretofore was unhesitatingly accorded to slavery and the
rights of the master."[23] These were prophetic words. The
fabric of the American federal order is being put to a severe
test. The degree of enforcement of civil rights legislation will
determine to what extent federal realities can be brought into
harmony with constitutional and statutory norms.

This federal reality has been further elucidated by a recent
"theory of confederacies."[24] In this interesting contribution,
C. J. Hughes argues that federal governments had "borrowed"
from confederacies the devices for protecting local cultures,
but that such confederacies made "the preservation of this
machinery itself part of the purpose." He believes that a true
theory of confederacies is easier to formulate than one of federations, and that such confederacy is "a true form of government with identifiable institutions." These appear to be (a)
a constitution, termed a treaty, (b) a council of ministers exercising the princely power in the center, possessing *de facto*
the power to overrule the objections of minor states, (c) a
body of officials identifying itself with the central power, and
(d) an authoritarian kind of government in the component
units. He believes that with the drift toward strong executives, confederacy is once more possible. This theory marks in
fact a return to the old dichotomy of federalism in terms of
sovereignty, though in weakened form. The federalizing process is here rigidified into a "decision" between a confederacy
and a federal system, which Hughes goes so far as to declaim
as "no form of government at all [and which] exists more in
the mind of the beholders than in the real world." Men living

in federal regimes would be startled to hear such a dictum.
Yet, it is important to develop the theory that an international federal scheme is a kind of government (see chapter
10). The same theme animates another recent study which includes the United Nations under the heading of international
federalism, coining for it the suggestive term "amphictyonic
federalism." Dusan Sidjanski has shown the truly federal
tendencies in such organizations as the Council of Europe
and has rightly emphasized the federalizing process which
they signalize.[25]

At the other end of the spectrum of federalism there has
emerged an increasing recognition of the fact that a federal
structure may be the result of a basic decision by a constituent
power to embody federal features as a species of separation of
powers in a constitutional charter.[26] It has been presented by
Konrad Hesse as the theory of the "unitary federal state."[27]
Proceeding from the very specific and concrete issues of German constitutional law, though Brazil, India, Nigeria, and a
number of other states would have served equally well, the
author argued that the Federal Republic is such a state. There
can be no question in such a regime of a compact or federal
"bargain." The constituent assembly of the Federal Republic, according to this view, decided in favor of federalism as an
organizational principle. He would call it the "federal principle" as contrasted with the "federalistic principle." In radical opposition to the conclusions of Hughes, Hesse would
assert that the federal principle is vital, while the federalistic
principle is obsolete. The former is, so he claims, a principle
of organization which a democratic people may adopt as a
suitable form of organization. This principle not only en-
larges the division of power, but it also affects the relation of
government and opposition, the structure and working of
parties and interest groups, and so forth. For Germany, Hesse
concludes that "a federal structure seems indispensable for
the free democratic order."[28] But by his preoccupation with
Germany's problems, he is led to overlook the possibility that

such a "basic decision" may, as seems to be the case in India, unloosen a federalizing process by giving scope to differentiations which eventually will demand more effective recognition, or achieve it as a result of other pressures, as was the case in Prussia.

One might, in this connection, suggest that the idea of a unitary federal state also has meaning in its application to totalitarian regimes such as the Soviet Union. For there, a unitary and unified party which claims to be the sole legitimate representative of the working people really does decide, in the interest of fulfilling its historical role as defined in the ideology of the movement, to adopt the structure and machinery of a federal state. But the key purpose is not, as the case of Yugoslavia also shows, the establishment of a division of power, but rather the satisfaction of cultural and linguistic needs which do not otherwise matter.[29]

We conclude this brief review of some recent theoretical trends and issues by stating that the basic insight, now increasingly accepted, is that federations of states and the federal state must be seen as particular applications of a recurrent form of effective organized cooperation between groups. A federal order is a union of group selves, united by one or more common objectives, a community of communities which retain their distinctive group being. It unites without destroying the selves that are uniting, and is meant to strengthen them in their group and communal relations. Thus, it is the particular relation which exists in fact that should shape the federal relationship. This relationship needs to be shaped, and is in fact so shaped in successful federalizing, in such a way that it can be reshaped and transformed in an ongoing process. That process may lead to greater unity or to greater diversity, and the federal bond will become weaker or stronger in response to it. In any case, it is clear that the small state and the small political community can only hope to survive in a world of ever widening contacts and interests[30] if federalism is recognized not as a panacea but as a useful instrumentality for good government. It remains to suggest once more that federalism also holds out the prospect of organizing the world at large, lest it be accomplished by imperial conquest and domination. Let us therefore conclude with a statement by John Stuart Mill: "When the conditions exist for the formation of efficient and durable federal unions, the multiplication of them is always a benefit to the world."[31] Thus the author of *Representative Government* foresaw, more than a hundred years ago, what has since been proven by political experience.

NOTES TO CHAPTER 23

1. The dynamic political view of federalism is becoming accepted so widely that it is beginning to appear in casual references. Thus we read in Héraud, *op. cit.* (note 1, chapter 4), p. 257, "Ce schéma est impliqué dans tout processus fédéralisant à base de traité . . . ."; and Cole, *op. cit.* (note 8, chapter 4), p. 62, writes: "Federalism is the process by which adjustment is made between those forces making for disunity and those making for unity."

2. See the highly formalistic presentation of A. I. Lepeshkin, "Problems of the development of the Soviet Socialist Federation," a paper read at IPSA (Geneva Congress, 1964). See contra, Beyme, *op. cit.* (note 14, chapter 22).

3. See Christa Altenstetter, *Der Föderalismus in Österreich, 1864–1965* (1968).

4. For Nigeria, see Robert O. Tilman and Taylor Cole (eds.), *The Nigerian Political Scene* (1962), chapter 3, by T. Cole, and Kalu Ezera, *Constitutional Developments in Nigeria* (1960), especially chapter X and pp. 248–49.

5. For the Caribbean, see James Fraser, *Centrifugalism in the Caribbean* (1968).

6. McWhinney, *op. cit.* (note 11, chapter 22), chapter 7, offers an explicit treatment of federal loyalty (*Bundestreue*) under the heading of "federal comity." Another able recent treatment is in Hay, *op. cit.* (note 11, chapter 10), pp. 194–201, where the more accurate translation "fidelity" is used.

7. The study by Englehart, *op. cit.* (note 2, chapter 6) offers some interesting data, as do many of the country studies of working federal regimes.

8. *Constitutional Government and Politics* (1937), p. 176.

9. *Ibid.*, p. 184. Instead of the word "league" the term confederation is used.

10. In the papers cited above (note 1, chapter 1), I overstated the issue by insisting that the dynamic aspect of federalizing replace the static aspect of patterning and structuring; I believe the present formulation to be more appropriate. For a more recent statement, see my article cited in note 1, chapter 11.

11. *Man and His Government* (1963), chapter 32.

12. Besides the works referred to above (note 6), some country studies are

highly suggestive. See also, for example, Denis de Rougemont, *La Suisse: ou L'Histoire d'un Peuple Heureux* (1965), *L'Europe dans le Monde* (1965); see also A. Marc (with Robert Aron), *Principes du Fédéralisme* (1954). These and other writers stressing the humanist and consensual aspect of federalism hark back to Proudhon, Constantin Franz, and Otto von Gierke.

13. An interesting instance is offered by Léo Moulin, *op. cit.* (note 11, chapter 3), chapter IX, "L'Ordre de Saint-Bénoît et les problèmes du fédéralisme."

14. Kenneth C. Wheare (note 10, chapter 1); Edward McWhinney, *Comparative Federalism—States' Rights and National Power* (1962); Bowie and Friedrich (eds.), *op. cit.* (note 1, chapter 1).

15. Wheare, *op. cit.*, pp. 32–33.

16. Wheare, *op. cit.*, chapter XII, pages 252–60.

17. Héraud, *op. cit.* (note 1, chapter 4). On page 260, one reads "L'aliénation économique et l'aliénation culturelle sont à cet égard les maux essentiels à surmonter," and it is federalism which can accomplish this.

18. Héraud, *op. cit.*, pp. 269, 266 ff. He develops the idea of the *fédération des ethnies.*

19. Héraud, *op. cit.*, p. 18, describes in vivid terms the loss of identity suffered by the member of an ethnic minority if he seeks to become effective in the larger community, how he must substitute for his original personality by great effort and sacrifice another—a veritable betrayal of his self.

20. McWhinney, *op. cit.* (note 14 above), p. 13.

21. Riker, *op. cit.* (note 6, chapter 5), p. 155. This author gingerly asserts that Wheare "displays very little understanding of political realities," but it would seem that Wheare stated the point more effectively and based it upon a richer knowledge of federal realities.

22. See Burke Marshall, *Federalism and Civil Rights* (1964), pp. 8–9.

23. *Ibid.*, pp. 83–84. For the general problem, see also *Transcendent Justice—The Religious Dimension of Constitutionalism* (1964), chapter 5.

24. Christopher Hughes, *Confederacies,* an inaugural address (1963).

25. Dusan Sidjanski, *Fédéralisme Amphictyonique—Éléments de Système et tendance internationale* (1956).

26. The territorial or spatial division of power was stressed in my *op. cit.* (note 8 above), chapter XI, entitled "Federalism and the Territorial Division of Power." I first brought forward this aspect in *Constitutional Government and Politics* (1937). This important theoretical point was further developed by *Area and Power, A Theory of Local Government,* ed. Arthur Maass (1959), with papers on the history of this aspect of federal theory by Stanley Hoffman and Samuel P. Huntington.

27. See Hesse, *op. cit.* (note 10, chapter 14). The argument tends to merge with that for local self-government.

28. Hesse, *op. cit.*, p. 32.

29. Lepeshkin, *op. cit.* (note 2 above); see also our study cited in note 12, chapter 22.

30. Sir J. A. R. Marriott, *Federalism and the Problem of the Small State* (1943). See in this connection also an interesting special study by Hassan Saab, *The Arab Federalists of the Ottoman Empire* (Amsterdam, 1958).

31. John Stuart Mill, *Considerations on Representative Government* (1861; Liberal Arts Press ed. 1958), chapter 17, p. 246.

INDEX

Adenauer, Konrad, 65
Administration, delegated, 70–74, 129–34; advantages of, 73
Africa, nationalism in, 31
African states, association of, 92
Althusius, Johannes, 12, 17, 20, 26, 27–28 n.
Amending power, need for, 90, 96 n.
American Commonwealth, The, 22
Aquinas, St. Thomas, 13
Aristotle, 12
Articles of Confederation (U.S.), 11–12, 14–15
Assam, 139
Australia, 18; cabinet in, 102–4; constitution of, 100–101; Democratic Labor Party of, 101; federal administration in, 72; federalism in, 99–105; Governor General of, 101; legislative system in, 101–2, 103; Loan Council in, 104; parliamentarianism in, 99–105; party system in, 63, 103; Prime Minister of, 101, 102, 104; social structure of, 55; states and territories of, 100
Australian Capital Territory, 100
Austria: and corporate federalism, 124; decentralization in, 7; and EEC, 91; and federal association, 95; federalism in, 174; and State Treaty (1955), 95; and Trentino, 145
Austria-Hungary, 5
Autonomy, 8

Basic Law (Federal Republic of Germany), 48, 62, 130, 131

Basic Principles (Yugoslavia), 163
Bavaria, 71, 129
Belgium: bilingualism in, 106, 107–8; and Community of the Six, 156; and constitution of 1831, 106; and Council of Europe, 156–57; and EEC, 107; federalism in, 30, 106–10; minorities in, 60; nationalism in, 31, 33; party system in, 50, 108
Benelux countries, 107; and Community of the Six, 156; and Council of Europe, 156–57
Berlin and federal association, 89, 93, 95
Bern, 149, 153
Bihar, 139
Bilingualism: in Belgium, 106, 107–8; in Canada, 116–18
Bill of Rights (U.S.), 19–20
Bismarck, Otto von, 160
Boccaccio, Giovanni, 31
Bodin, Jean, 12
Bolzano, 146
Bombay, 139
Bowie, R. R., 9 n., 178
Brabant, 107
Brazil: and constitution of 1946, 112; federalism in, 111–15; social structure in, 112–14
British Columbia, 120
British Commonwealth: and common citizenship, 86–87; as international federalism, 83; planning in, 44; Prime Ministers' Conference, 84, 93; and supranationalism, 82
British Empire, 83
British North America Act (1867), 119

187